Raising a Digital Child

A Digital Citizenship Handbook for Parents

Mike Ribble

HomePage Books

HomePage Books is an imprint of the
International Society for Technology in Education

EUGENE, OREGON • WASHINGTON, DC

Raising a Digital Child
A Digital Citizenship Handbook for Parents

Mike Ribble

Director of Book Publishing: *Courtney Burkholder*
Acquisitions Editor: *Jeff V. Bolkan*
Production Editors: *Lynda Gansel, Lanier Brandau*
Production Coordinator: *Rachel Bannister*
Graphic Designer and Book Design: *Signe Landin*

Rights and Permissions
   Administrator: *Lanier Brandau*
Developmental and
   Copy Editor: *Lynne Ertle*
Book Production: *Tracy Cozzens*

Library of Congress Cataloging-in-Publication Data

Ribble, Mike.
  Raising a digital child : a digital citizenship handbook for parents /
Mike Ribble. — 1st ed.
    p. cm.
  Includes bibliographical references.
  ISBN 978-1-56484-250-3 (pbk.)
  1. Computers and children. 2. Internet and children. 3. Digital media. 4. Education—Parent participation.   I. Title.
  QA76.9.C659R53 2009
  302.23'1—dc22

2008051444

First Edition
ISBN: 978-1-56484-250-3
Printed in the United States of America

HomePage Books is an imprint of the International Society for Technology in Education. The HomePage Books name and logo are trademarks of the International Society for Technology in Education.

International Society for Technology in Education (ISTE)
Washington, DC, Office:
   1710 Rhode Island Ave. NW, Suite 900, Washington, DC 20036-3132
Eugene, Oregon, Office:
   180 West 8th Ave., Suite 300, Eugene, OR 97401-2916
Order Desk: 1.800.336.5191
Order Fax: 1.541.302.3778
Customer Service: orders@iste.org
Book Publishing: books@iste.org
Rights and Permissions: permissions@iste.org
Web: www.iste.org

Cover photo (bottom right): © iStockphoto.com/Bonnie Jacobs

About ISTE

The International Society for Technology in Education (ISTE) is the trusted source for professional development, knowledge generation, advocacy, and leadership for innovation. A nonprofit membership association, ISTE provides leadership and service to improve teaching, learning, and school leadership by advancing the effective use of technology in PK–12 and teacher education.

Home of the National Educational Technology Standards (NETS), the Center for Applied Research in Educational Technology (CARET), and the National Educational Computing Conference (NECC), ISTE represents more than 100,000 professionals worldwide. We support our members with information, networking opportunities, and guidance as they face the challenge of transforming education. To find out more about these and other ISTE initiatives, visit our website at **www.iste.org**.

As part of our mission, ISTE Book Publishing works with experienced educators to develop and produce practical resources for classroom teachers, teacher educators, technology leaders, and parents. Every manuscript we select for publication is professionally edited. We look for content that emphasizes the effective use of technology where it can make a difference—both at school and at home. We value your feedback on this book and other ISTE products. E-mail us at **books@iste.org**.

About the Author

Mike Ribble has worked at several different levels of education. He has served as a classroom biology teacher, a secondary school administrator, a network manager for a community college, and a university instructor. He received a doctorate in educational leadership at Kansas State University. His interests include technology leadership, professional development, and working with teachers to help enhance teaching and learning with technology. He has written several articles and has presented at regional and national conferences on digital citizenship and its effect on the changes within education.

Contents

Digital Citizen Creed

As a technological society it is our responsibility to provide the opportunity to work, interact, and use technology without the interference, obstruction, or destruction by the actions of inappropriate technology users. As digital citizens, we pledge to help create a society that strives to use technology appropriately. We will work with others to identify the needs of technology users and to meet those needs.

The following nine elements form the basis for appropriate technology use. These elements provide a starting place to help all technology users understand the fundamentals of digital citizenship. There is no way to predict what the future holds for us in terms of new technologies, but we can lay the foundation now for appropriate use. By becoming more aware of the issues related to technology, everyone can become better digital citizens.

Digital Access: full electronic participation in society

> *Can all technology users participate in a digital society at acceptable levels if they choose?*

Digital Commerce: the buying and selling of goods online

> *Do technology users have the knowledge and protection to buy and sell in a digital world?*

Digital Communication: the electronic exchange of information

> *Is there an understanding of the various digital communication methods and when each is appropriate?*

Digital Literacy: the capability to use digital technology and knowing when and how to use it

> *Have technology users taken the time to learn about various digital technologies and when their use is appropriate?*

Digital Etiquette: the standards of conduct expected by other digital technology users

> *Do technology users consider others when using digital technologies?*

Digital Law: the legal rights and restrictions governing technology use

> *Are technology users aware of rules, policies, or laws that govern the use of digital technologies?*

Digital Rights and Responsibilities: the privileges and freedoms extended to all digital technology users, and the behavioral expectations that come with them

> *Are technology users ready to protect the rights of others and to defend their own digital rights?*

Digital Health and Wellness: the elements of physical and psychological well-being related to digital technology use

> *Do technology users consider the risks (both physical and psychological) when using digital technologies?*

Digital Security: the precautions that all technology users must take to guarantee their personal safety and the security of their network

> *Do technology users work to protect their own information and that of others?*

These nine elements and their core questions form the backbone of digital citizenship. If we are to be effective users of technology we must act in appropriate ways, as well as teach others the proper behavior. These should be the duties of all digital citizens.

Introduction

Technology is all around us. Children today are bombarded with the messages that they must be a part of this new digital culture. At an increasingly younger age each year, children ask for cell phones, e-mail, and instant messaging (IM) accounts. Parents are placed in what seems like a no-win situation. If you deny your children the use of these digital technologies, your children may be left behind. But if you allow your children to have access, you must cope with paying for the technology, cyberbullying, and online stalking, just to name a few issues. So what is a parent to do?

You first need to be aware of the digital technologies that your children encounter every day. You also must understand the potential problems and risks, and how to reduce the chances that your children might run into trouble. For many parents these might seem to be overwhelming tasks, especially with new technologies appearing at an alarming rate. Parents need a structure for coping with and behaving in this new digital society. The framework presented in this book is called digital citizenship.

What is digital citizenship? Put simply, *digital citizenship means using technology appropriately and responsibly.* What it is not is a set of rules that must be followed. Rather, a foundation in digital citizenship helps parents (and their children) to recognize what is and what is not appropriate technology use.

What's Inside This Book

This book is intended as an introduction to digital citizenship for parents. Each of the nine elements will be discussed in detail—along with a host of technology issues—and suggestions are provided for teaching it at home. The discussion is organized into three sections with a total of eight chapters, followed by four appendixes.

Section 1: Understanding Digital Citizenship

Section 1 sets the groundwork for understanding digital citizenship. Chapter 1 introduces the topic and encourages you to jump right in with an exercise called the 21st-Century Digital Compass Activity. This activity addresses some of the technology issues that arise every day. Chapter 2 provides definitions for the nine elements along with suggestions for thinking about the topics and talking about them with your kids.

Section 2: Bringing Digital Citizenship into the Home

Section 2 provides the toolkit for working with your kids. Is downloading music an issue in your household, or cyberbullying? Chapter 3 helps you decide where to focus your attention. It organizes the nine elements into three categories. Chapter 4 introduces the Cycle of Technology Use, a process that promotes lifelong skills that can be applied to any new technologies. Chapter 5 contains two questionnaires to help you find out what your kids know. Once you're aware of the weak spots in their knowledge, you'll know where to focus your efforts.

Section 3: Digital Citizenship for Everyone

In the book *The World Is Flat*, Thomas Friedman talks about the changes that are happening in our world. It is not enough to simply think about your children's career prospects in the country they grew up in. You must also be aware that as adults they will be competing for jobs with people from around the world. We all need to be conscious of this new global perspective, and this section attempts to broaden your outlook. Chapter 6 takes a hard look at current trends in technology use. The facts presented show that technology use problems at home and at school are also found at work and in other areas of society. Chapter 7 talks about the development of Web 2.0 and the potential problems of social networking on the Internet. Chapter 8 brings it all together with concluding material.

Appendixes

Several appendixes have been made available for further reference. Appendix A provides definitions of terms relevant to digital citizenship. In Appendixes B and C you will find quick-start ideas for introducing the ideas of digital citizenship to your family. Appendix B lists several technologies and offers suggestions for ensuring their appropriate use in the home. Appendix C contains a family contract for digital citizenship, with both a kid's pledge and a parent's pledge. The contract covers the topics embodied in the nine elements of digital citizenship. Appendix D lists the National Educational Technology Standards for Students (NETS•S), which may be used in your children's schools.

Source

Thomas Friedman. (2005). *The world is flat.* New York: Farrar, Straus, and Giroux.

Searching for Further Information

This book does not provide lists of websites for you to explore. Websites tend to disappear without notification, and new, often better, information is posted regularly. Rather, I have provided a list of keywords in Chapter 2. Parents can use these keywords when searching for additional information on the Internet.

If you are unsure of how to search effectively, instructions and helpful tips for building basic and advanced searches are available from search engine sites such as the following:

- Google's Web Search Help Center: www.google.com/support/?ctx=Web

- Yahoo! Search: http://tools.search.yahoo.com/about/

- MSN Web Search Help: http://search.msn.com/docs/help.aspx

- Ask.com Advanced Search Tips: http://help.ask.com/en/docs/about/adv_search_tips.shtml

Although each search engine offers different options for searching, most advanced searches involve common Boolean operators. These operators allow you to broaden or narrow your search. The following chart lists common operators and provides examples for using them.

Operator	Description	Example
AND, +, &	include both words	digital AND divide
OR, |	include either word	digital OR technology AND access
NOT, -	exclude this word	digital NOT continental AND divide
AND NOT, !	all but this word	spam AND NOT Hormel
NEAR, ~	looks for words similar to this word; good for misspellings	NEAR phishing
*	wildcard; includes plurals and close matches	ergonomic*
" "	looks for the exact words or phrase within the quote marks	"digital dirt road divide"
title:, t:	looks for the word in the title of the page	title: digital divide
url:, u:	looks for the word in the URL	u: spyware
define:	finds definitions of words	define: spyware

Go ahead and check out these search engines and try the various features. A world of information will open up before you. How can you tell if the information is valid? The digital literacy extra in Chapter 2 provides five guidelines for evaluating websites. With just a little practice, you'll become an old hand at locating Internet resources and winnowing down the selection to the very best. Remember that learning is not a single step, but a journey. Enjoy the opportunities that technology provides, and help others as well.

Understanding
Digital Citizenship

May you live in interesting times.
—Chinese proverb and curse

This saying seems to fit very well with where we are with technology today. We do live in interesting times, but we need to decide what "interesting" means.

Does interesting mean, as the saying implies, a time of chaos? Perhaps it does. We are in a time of much change, and technology is in large part the cause of this change. In just the last two decades we have seen the growth of the Internet from the playground of a few to the way many of us gather our information each day.

Technologies can spring up, evolve into new forms, and become obsolete very quickly. These certainly can be considered chaotic times.

Or does interesting mean something much different? Are these times providing us a new way to look at the world around us? Our children are growing up with experiences that in many ways are very different from our own. They have access to information we never dreamed of. If information is power, then this generation has the potential to be one of the most powerful generations in the history of humanity. But with power comes responsibility. We need to show our children how to harness this information in an appropriate way.

This section provides an introduction to digital citizenship. Chapter 1 examines the importance of teaching kids appropriate technology use and working with our schools and communities to promote responsible behavior. The 21st-Century Digital Compass Activity encourages you to dive right into the challenges of the Digital Age. Chapter 2 explores the nine elements of digital citizenship and their accompanying issues.

Getting Started

When I talk to parents about how their children use technology, parents often throw up their hands and say, "They know about this stuff and we don't" or "How can we monitor something that we don't understand?" Parents hear about all the negative things that are going on with kids and technology through the media—sharing personal information with strangers, illegally downloading music and movies, bullying others through e-mail and social networking sites. Parents ask themselves, "Didn't we raise our children to know better than this?" Of course, more often than not the answer is *yes*. We taught our kids to do the right thing, just as we were taught—look both ways before crossing the street, don't talk to strangers, don't steal candy from the grocery store. But we haven't taught them enough. We are working with a generation that has the awesome power of mass communication, but that has not learned the basics of digital citizenship.

Parents need to be involved in the process of raising their children to be good digital citizens. Fortunately, more parents than ever are trying to understand what their children are doing with technology. Research suggests that a majority of parents are taking action to protect their children when using technology. For example, some parents have installed software to block objectionable websites. The problem is, kids can find ways to get around these barriers. It is not enough to try to block out the problems around us. We need to teach our children how to live and work in this new digital society.

There are many technology issues that parents need to be aware of to help their children become effective adults. And today, with the rise of technology use, being able to talk with your children about these issues is important. Children are bombarded with conflicting messages when it comes to technology use, so it is up to adults, parents in particular, to help children understand what they need to know. We cannot be angry at our children (or others) for the way they use technology inappropriately if we have not taught them what we consider appropriate. But to help children, parents must understand what the issues are, not just with the Internet, but with all technologies.

The digital world is growing and changing very fast. Technology companies release products so rapidly that there is little time for anyone to stop and think of issues that might arise with their use. Too often when we purchase a new digital technology we look at all the bells and whistles and don't think of the consequences or all the potential misuses of the technology.

In the year 2000 we hadn't even begun thinking about social networking sites, but now they are discussed everywhere in mainstream media. Parenting the "MySpace Generation" involves completely new protocols from the ones most parents grew up with, not to mention new ways of understanding the world. For example, some are concerned that technology tends to isolate people—kids text each other instead of talking face-to-face. On the other hand, technology enables people to communicate with millions of others around the globe in seconds.

This concept of being alone, yet visible to anyone online, can be difficult for children to comprehend. Often, because children do not see others while they work and play online, they believe they are anonymous. They post personal information online because they don't believe that anyone other than their friends would care about it. Unfortunately, they are wrong. People might be watching their conversations. Digital technology also offers a wall to hide behind. Sometimes people use this anonymity to write hateful e-mails and posts because the recipient is not standing in front of them. How often have we hit the Send button only to think of the ramifications afterward?

Technology offers exciting opportunities, but for some parents this strange new world can be scary. Every day we see articles and news programs about online stalkers, pedophiles, college admissions offices, and potential employers checking up on our kids online. How is a parent to keep up with the issues when there are so many to think about?

This is where digital citizenship comes in. It provides a framework for understanding appropriate technology use. The nine elements of digital citizenship can help parents see the larger picture related to technology. These elements do not focus just on the Internet or other technologies, but allow for a broader perspective of technology use, misuse, and abuse.

Elements of Digital Citizenship

Digital citizenship is a new way to think about digital technologies. Instead of focusing on what technology can do, the aim is to think about how technology should be used. As defined in the introduction, digital citizenship means using technology appropriately and responsibly.

This book on digital citizenship is not simply a list of rules. Instead, it offers ideas and guidelines for thinking about technology. Here are the reasons why:

- It is better for someone to be involved in the process of doing the right thing.

- Technology changes so quickly that today's rules may not be applicable tomorrow.

- What is right for one family may not be right for others.

I have identified nine elements within the broader concept of digital citizenship: digital access, digital commerce, digital communication, digital literacy, digital etiquette, digital law, digital rights and responsibilities, digital health and wellness, and digital security.

Within the nine elements there is a fair amount of overlap of issues and ideas. For example, the topic of cell phones can easily fit into discussions of digital communication, digital etiquette, and digital health and wellness. All of the elements need to be kept in mind when thinking about appropriate technology use. When reading through the nine elements in Chapter 2, you and your children should discuss how each element affects you and how you can apply the concepts to your own use of technology. The process of learning how to think about technology and use it appropriately is discussed in greater depth in Chapter 4.

Digital Citizenship in Schools

It is the responsibility of parents, educators, and members of the community to provide children with an understanding of what it means to live and work in a digital society. Schools and independent educational organizations are increasingly recognizing the importance of digital citizenship.

The International Society for Technology in Education (ISTE) has developed the National Educational Technology Standards (NETS) for students, teachers, and administrators. With these standards, ISTE provides structure for using technology in a responsible way. In 2007, the NETS for Students (NETS•S) were updated, replacing the standard of Social, Ethical, and Human Issues with the new standard of Digital Citizenship to encompass the ideas of ethics in an educational setting. The NETS are used in every U.S. state and many countries, demonstrating the importance of technology standards as a part of the educational curricula. See Appendix D for a full listing of the NETS for Students.

It is up to parents to ask educators if they are teaching digital citizenship at school. Find out whether the teachers in your school district consider responsible technology use a priority or believe it is an important skill for our children's future.

Source

International Society for Technology in Education (ISTE). (No date). *National educational technology standards.* Retrieved June 17, 2008, from www.iste.org/nets/

It Takes a Village

Digital citizenship is not for just one person or one group of technology users. Everyone belonging to this new digital society has a part to play, including understanding the issues surrounding technology use. Why is it so important to understand these issues? Because we are all teachers, whether we realize it or not. Anyone who passes on information to another is educating that person. This is the basis behind the statement that "it takes a village to raise a child."

Parents hope that their children will be able to learn what they need and differentiate what is right and what is wrong. However, without the basic knowledge of digital citizenship, children may not think of the consequences of their actions. People often think that the way they use technology has no effect on others, but this is simply not the case. Not only could their actions be inconveniencing others, but they may be modeling behaviors that other people, including children, will observe and emulate. Without the knowledge of appropriate technology use as well as a certain level of self-awareness, irresponsible behavior and bad habits can be passed along. However, if we take the concept of digital citizenship into our workplaces and communities, we can set a new standard of how we (and hopefully others) will act with respect to technology. We can pass on good behavior by showing others that we have certain guidelines for technology use. We all need to step up to the plate and be good role models, not just at home, but in our communities.

Remember that what you teach your children today is what they will be teaching their children in the future. But you're not in it alone. Digital citizenship is about addressing technology issues as a community. We all need to work together to mold the digital society we envision for future generations.

The 21st-Century Digital Compass Activity

The 21st-Century Digital Compass Activity can help determine the direction of both you and your child in relation to appropriate technology use. Read the following scenarios and come up with your own answers. Then read the descriptions of the six points on the compass to determine which direction you are going (see the Digital Compass figure). You may have a different direction for each scenario. Then go ahead and look at the guidelines in the section called Interpreting the Answers.

After you are finished, have your child go through the same process to determine his or her direction. See if your child's answers match yours. If the answers do not match, have your child explain how he or she may see the issues differently than you do. The goal of this activity is not to determine one correct answer for each scenario (although in some cases that may be quite clear), but to open lines of discussion about appropriate technology use.

Don't worry if you feel unsure about your own answers at this point. You may be more comfortable with this activity after you've read Chapter 2 and familiarized yourself with the nine elements. This activity does, however, provide an introduction to some of the technology issues we see today, so it is well worth a look.

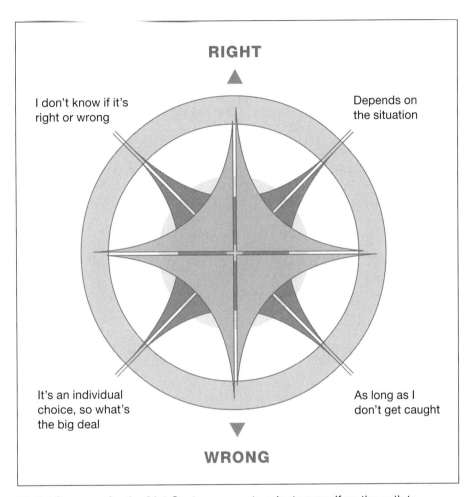

Digital Compass for the 21st Century, a way to orient yourself on the path to digital citizenship

Scenario 1. One person sends a harassing e-mail to another person. The receiver retaliates with a "flaming e-mail." *Is sending harassing and flaming e-mail messages wrong?*

Scenario 2. When going to the movies, a person gets a cell phone call and conducts a loud conversation. *Is talking in a loud voice on a mobile phone in a public place acceptable behavior?*

Scenario 3. A person logs on to a P2P (peer-to-peer) file-sharing website and downloads the newest song. *Is downloading music from P2P sites wrong?*

Scenario 4. A person clicks on an unknown link to a website and downloads a virus to the home computer. *Should users have some knowledge of where they are going before they click?*

Scenario 5. The night before an assignment is due for a class, a student goes to a website and copies and pastes information without giving credit to the author. *Is using Internet materials without giving credit to the author wrong?*

Scenario 6. A person uses a software package to copy movies and games from DVDs for friends. *Is copying copyrighted materials right?*

Scenario 7. A student goes online to a school website to download material she needs for class. *Is online learning appropriate for grade school, middle school, or high school students?*

Scenario 8. Two people are text messaging on their cell phones to gossip about someone else. *Is it appropriate to send text messages about others?*

Scenario 9. A person creates and publishes a website on the Internet for personal use, but the website cannot be read by people with disabilities. *Is it right to make websites that are not accessible to people with disabilities?*

Scenario 10. A technology user is given a USB flash drive by a friend with lots of different files on it. The technology user does not check what is on the drive before installing the files. *Is it appropriate to connect a storage device with unknown files to any computer?*

Scenario 11. A technology user places a keystroke logging program on a computer to get passwords or other information. *Is putting programs on a computer without another's knowledge appropriate?*

Evaluating Your Child's Answers

There is no easy answer for any of the scenarios, and responses will vary. Why? Many situations have shades of gray, and even technology users with a strong foundation in digital citizenship may have different "right" answers. When interpreting each scenario, consider not only your own background and experience, but how others might see it. The purpose of the compass activity is to help children and their parents analyze their ideas about appropriate technology use. Use the following six compass directions to interpret the answers.

Wrong. When technology users travel in the wrong direction, the cause is often bad information, lack of training, or a lack of consideration for others. To get back on the right path, children need to learn how their technology use can affect others.

It's an individual choice, so what's the big deal? Often children don't consider how others may feel about their behavior, and they believe "if it doesn't bother me, why should it bother anyone else?" Children traveling in this direction can't understand what the big fuss is about. Parents need to help their children see beyond their own personal needs. As technology becomes more personalized and accessible, it becomes a part of who we are. Children may say, "Because my cell phone is mine, what I do with it is my concern." Some children believe that technology use is a right and not a privilege. Simply put, they don't want others to tell them how to use their technology.

As long as I don't get caught. Children choosing this direction believe that technology is there to be used, and even if they do something questionable, everything will be fine as long as no one else knows. The trouble with this attitude is that what we do or don't do can and often does affect others around us. Many children know that what they are doing is not right, but they believe that if no one knows, that makes it acceptable.

Depends on the situation. Different situations may call for different behavior, but an overarching understanding of appropriate technology use is still important. Children need to know that some activities may be appropriate in one situation but not in another.

I don't know if it's right or wrong. Some children are given technology but fail to learn how to use it appropriately. However, ignorance cannot be used as a defense for technology misuse or abuse. Basic digital citizenship skills should be learned in addition to simply learning how to use the technology. This is the direction people go when they understand some aspects of technology but "only enough to be dangerous." Sometimes, this can be worse than having no training at all. When no digital citizenship training is provided, children learn from others and can get poor advice.

Right. Traveling in the right direction takes time and diligence. To follow this path, children need to have a good understanding of the technology they are using. They also need to reflect on how they use technology on a daily basis. Those who follow the right direction take time to decide not only how their actions affect themselves, but those around them.

Most of the instances of going in a wrong direction stem from a lack of understanding about how our actions affect others. Chapter 4 suggests ways to build awareness of our individual technology use.

Interpreting the Answers

Scenario 1. One person sends a harassing e-mail to another person. The receiver retaliates with a "flaming e-mail." *Is sending harassing and flaming e-mail messages wrong?*

> **Answer guidelines.** While most adults would see sending a harassing e-mail to another person as wrong, some children might say that it's OK as long as they don't get caught, or perhaps that it depends on the situation. If your child provides this kind of answer, you might probe deeper. How would they respond verbally to the same situation? The feeling of anonymity (not seeing the other person) may add to the motivation to respond in a negative manner, as well as support the idea that they may not get caught.

Scenario 2. When going to the movies, a person gets a cell phone call and conducts a loud conversation. *Is talking in a loud voice on a mobile phone in a public place acceptable behavior?*

> **Answer guidelines.** Cell phone use has become second nature for many people, and we often forget that we are talking loudly in a public place. Even though establishments such as movie theaters and houses of worship remind us, we still sometimes forget. Some children may respond that it's the individual's choice or that they don't know if it's right or wrong.

Scenario 3. A person logs on to a P2P (peer-to-peer) file-sharing website and downloads the newest song. *Is downloading music from P2P sites wrong?*

> **Answer guidelines.** With the easy access to P2P sites and the simplicity of downloading songs from these sites (without being informed of the possible legal issues), many users may not know if it is right or wrong. Those who do know that they could be charged with illegal downloading may respond that it's OK as long as they don't get caught.

Scenario 4. A person clicks on an unknown link to a website and downloads a virus to the home computer. *Should users have some knowledge of where they are going before they click?*

Answer guidelines. Many technology users are unaware that just by visiting a website they risk infecting their computers with a virus, spyware, or adware. Many simply don't know if what they are doing is right or wrong. This is why technology users need to make sure that their antivirus, antispyware, and antiadware programs are installed and up-to-date.

Scenario 5. The night before an assignment is due for a class, a student goes to a website and copies and pastes information without giving credit to the author. *Is using Internet materials without giving credit to the author wrong?*

Answer guidelines. Many technology users have learned that taking information without the creator's permission is wrong. However, information on the Internet is easy to access and seems available for anyone to use, so some kids might think that it's OK to copy as long as they don't get caught or that it depends on the situation. Let your children know that people who provide the information might expect to be paid for their effort, or would at least like some credit for the work they have done. It would be even better to seek out the permission of the creator.

Scenario 6. A person uses a software package to copy movies and games from DVDs for friends. *Is copying copyrighted materials right?*

Answer guidelines. Almost all of us have seen the copyright notification at the beginning of movies that lets us know that it is wrong to make copies. Still, some people might believe that it's OK as long as they don't get caught or that it's an individual's choice. Some people might rationalize that the big companies make so much money that the one copy they make won't make a difference.

Scenario 7. A student goes online to a school website to download material she needs for class. *Is online learning appropriate for grade school, middle school, or high school students?*

> **Answer guidelines.** Making information available to students through the web has become very acceptable in our schools. Some parents may be hesitant to download materials (even from a school) if they are concerned about viruses, spyware, adware, and other dangers. If parents do not understand how these systems are configured they may not know if this activity is right or wrong. Parents need to work with educators to learn how these systems are to be used at home.

Scenario 8. Two people are text messaging on their cell phones to gossip about someone else. *Is it appropriate to send text messages about others?*

> **Answer guidelines.** Gossip in any form is usually seen as wrong, but people still do it. With the new technologies it has become easy to talk about others in various formats (through blogging, texting, and instant messaging). Your kids may see this as an individual choice or think it's OK as long as they don't get caught.

Scenario 9. A person creates and publishes a website on the Internet for personal use, but the website cannot be read by people with disabilities. *Is it right to make websites that are not accessible to people with disabilities?*

> **Answer guidelines.** Web publishing programs have made creating and uploading websites very easy. Often technology users do not think about the people who might look at their site. As web developers, they should think about others, but since the website is being created for personal use they may see this as an individual's choice. People who have not learned that creating accessible sites is even an option may not know if this is right or wrong.

Scenario 10. A technology user is given a USB flash drive by a friend with lots of different files on it. The technology user does not check what is on the drive before installing the files. *Is it appropriate to connect a storage device with unknown files to any computer?*

Answer guidelines. When a friend hands us a flash drive, we may not consider whether anything could be wrong with the files. Many of us take it on faith that the information has been checked out before it is given to us. Some might say it depends on the situation (some friends being more careful and responsible than others), while others may simply not know if it's right or wrong. As mentioned before, it is always important to make sure you have up-to-date antivirus, antispyware, and antiadware software.

Scenario 11. A technology user places a keystroke logging program on a computer to get passwords or other information. *Is putting programs on a computer without another's knowledge appropriate?*

Answer guidelines. Keystroke logging, or keylogging, programs can be used to gather information, such as finding the source of errors in computer systems or measuring employee productivity on clerical tasks. They can also be used to obtain passwords or encryption keys, which is useful in law enforcement and for less noble pursuits. Most users would believe that putting a keystroke logging or any other foreign program on another's computer is wrong, but some may feel that this would be acceptable as long as they don't get caught.

CHAPTER 2

What Parents
Need to Know

Over the last few years as I looked at the issues that surround technology, certain common themes kept showing up. After digging deeper into these themes, I began to develop the nine elements of digital citizenship.

Digital citizenship is not a new concept. If you search the Internet you will discover that other groups have been discussing digital citizenship for many years. However, there are some fundamental differences between these other discussions and my approach. Other digital citizenship discussions often focus on specific topics, such as the digital divide (some people have technology and some don't) or the illegal downloading of music. My approach is more expansive in nature. It includes these topics within the broader conceptual elements of digital access and digital law. Another difference is that other researchers place only three or four topics under the umbrella of digital citizenship. My approach describes nine separate elements. In looking at these other versions, it is evident that they do not provide parents with enough detail about what digital citizenship truly means.

As I went about my research, it became clear that we need a framework to understand what it means to be a digital citizen. Think back to when you were growing up. Your parents probably provided direction on how they wanted you to act as you went out into society. Raising children has been done this way for generations. Every so often a generation faces a major transition from one way of thinking to another. This is one of those transitional times. We are moving into a Digital Age, with more gray areas and fewer constraints. New technologies are popping up every day, with user manuals for mechanical functions but no guidelines for appropriate use. It is up to us to develop and adhere to those guidelines, to provide direction for our children.

The nine elements of digital citizenship can help provide the new direction, the new framework, for this generation. The elements give parents and children a common vocabulary for talking about the issues that surround us in this developing digital society. But like any society, the framework is only as good as those who support it. If people are not interested in or not willing to work to support these ideas, then they are not going to help us move on together. Here are the nine elements of digital citizenship and their definitions.

Digital Access: full electronic participation in society

Digital Commerce: the buying and selling of goods online

Digital Communication: the electronic exchange of information

Digital Literacy: the capability to use digital technology and knowing when and how to use it

Digital Etiquette: the standards of conduct expected by other digital technology users

Digital Law: the legal rights and restrictions governing technology use

Digital Rights and Responsibilities: the privileges and freedoms extended to all digital technology users, and the behavioral expectations that come with them

Digital Health and Wellness: the elements of physical and psychological well-being related to digital technology use

Digital Security: the precautions that all technology users must take to guarantee their personal safety and the security of their network

Each element is further explained later in this chapter, with emphasis on issues of concern to parents. What will become evident after reading the discussions is that there is a fair amount of overlap between the topics. Digital technologies do not typically do one thing, but often have many uses. For example, today you can buy cell phones that surf the web, send text messages, play music, take photographs and video, and of course make calls. We are often aware of the additional aspects of devices, but we don't necessarily think about them in the context of appropriate use. When you read through the nine elements, the variety of issues attached to even a single device will become clearer.

This book talks about issues that come up with many different technologies (such as the Internet, cell phones, MP3 players, and computers) to provide a wide coverage of current technology use topics. This book cannot, however, cover all the issues related to technology use and misuse. There's not enough space for that. Besides, as new technologies emerge and old ones find new uses (which happens almost daily anymore), new problems and concerns will arise. What this book does is provide a roadmap for understanding appropriate technology use, and those basic concepts can be applied to future technologies.

As you go through each element, ask yourself, "How does this affect my children and my family?" Broaden your thinking about technology and realize that there may be concerns you were not aware of before. Think of issues not listed in this book (which there will be) and how they could fit into the nine elements. If you are looking for direction with some of today's more popular technologies (such as MP3 players, gaming systems, or cell phones) refer to Appendix B.

Digital Access

DEFINITION: *Full electronic participation in society*

Parents today often want to make sure that their children have the same opportunities as their peers. One factor that causes the division between kids is technology. Early on, when technology was new, this separation was defined as the *digital divide*. This term is still used, but the issue has expanded. No longer are we talking about access to computers alone (which there are many more of today), but to other technologies as well. Previously, family income was a big factor in digital access. Now age is also a concern. Children as young as five and six are given cell phones and MP3 players. Kids are defining their friends by whether they can call them on a cell phone, send them an instant message (IM), or go to their social networking site (such as MySpace, Xanga, or Friendster). So what are you to do? Allow the access or simply deny it so that it is not an issue? And what of those children who do not have the opportunity to use these technologies? Will they be left behind?

Understanding digital access also includes being aware of people with disabilities who might want to use certain technologies. Technology is often created with the assumption that everyone has the same abilities. It is often created for the same gender, ethnicity, and ability as the people who designed it. There may be as much inequality with technology as there is in other aspects of society. While many hardware and software manufacturers provide opportunities for those with disabilities, some still overlook people with special needs. This insensitivity can generate feelings of exclusion or hostility among people with disabilities who would like to use the technology.

Technology users need to be aware that online, as well as in face-to-face society, not everyone is treated equally. With decreasing costs, technology is becoming more readily available to all, but there are still issues of equality that need to be addressed in a digital society.

Digital Access Topics

- Having regular access to technologies, such as a computer in the home

- Accommodating "other abilities" such as color blindness or sensitivity when viewing flashing websites

- Not providing high-speed connectivity because of location or financial factors

Thinking about Digital Access

- Some individuals may choose not to use digital technologies. Can you provide opportunities for everyone whether they have access or not?

- When creating anything that will be accessed digitally (such as a website) consider the different abilities or equipment of others who may want to experience it.

Talking to Your Children about Digital Access

- Do you know children who do not have computers, cell phones, or iPods? How do you (or others) treat them?

- Do you talk to your friends using a cell phone or computer (through instant messaging or e-mail)? Do you have any friends you can't contact with a cell phone or computer?

Digital Access Keywords

- digital dirt road divide

- digital divide

- technology access

- technology access and minorities

- technology and the disabled

Digital Access Extra

Real Access to Technology

With digital access, the concern is not only having the opportunity to use technology but also eliminating any barriers, such as time, location, or physical barriers. When there are too many barriers to technology use (such as people not understanding its purpose, being unable to easily make it work, or lacking the support needed to sustain its use) true access does not exist.

Ensuring digital access is beyond the ability of one group. Everyone needs to realize the issues and work together to come up with solutions that are workable for all users.

Bridges.org, an international organization that promotes the effective use of ICT (information and communication technology) in the developing world for meaningful purposes, has identified the following 12 factors that determine whether ICT can be effectively used by people:

- **Physical access.** Is technology available and accessible to people and organizations?

- **Appropriate technology.** Is the available technology appropriate to local needs and conditions? What is the appropriate technology according to how people need and want to put technology to use?

- **Affordability.** Is technology affordable for people to use?

- **Capacity.** Do people have the training and skills necessary for effective technology use? Do they understand how to use technology and its potential uses?

- **Relevant content.** Is locally relevant content available, especially in terms of language?

- **Integration.** Is technology use a burden to peoples' lives, or is it integrated into daily routines?

- **Sociocultural factors.** Are people limited in their use of technology based on gender, race, or other sociocultural factors?

- **Trust.** Do people have confidence in technology and understand the implications of the technology they use, for instance in terms of privacy, security, or cybercrime?

- **Legal and regulatory framework.** Do laws and regulations limit technology use? Are changes needed to create an environment that fosters its use?

- **Local economic environment.** Is there a local economic environment favorable to technology use? Is technology part of local economic development? What is needed to make it a part?

- **Macroeconomic environment.** Is technology use limited by the macroeconomic environment in the country or region, for example, in terms of deregulation, investment, and labor issues?

- **Political will.** Is there political will in government to do what is needed to enable the integration of technology throughout society, and public support for government decision-making?

Source

Teresa Peters, Executive Director. (2008). *Bridging the digital divide.* Bridges.org. Retrieved January 12, 2008, from http://usinfo.state.gov/journals/itgic/1103/ijge/gj08.htm Used with permission.

Digital Commerce

DEFINITION: *The buying and selling of goods online*

Technology has provided many benefits to commerce. Being able to go online, find what you are looking for, research multiple vendors, pick the lowest price, and have it sent directly to your home is a benefit to most technology users. Children see this opportunity and want to take advantage of it as well. But what children (and some adults) often do not see are the negative aspects of digital commerce.

One hot topic is identity theft. When people place personal information online where others can access it, identity theft can occur. It can be devastating, ruining credit and causing havoc for many years. Identity theft can happen in many ways, but you can protect yourself somewhat by being aware of a website's security measures for personal information.

Another issue is the growth of credit card debt. Because of the ease of buying online, it can quickly get out of hand. With just a click of a button, you can have anything you want, and children can spend more than they would if they had purchased the item from a brick-and-mortar business.

Online auctions are a contributing factor to credit card debt. Online auction houses, such as eBay, are inviting to kids because of the number and types of items available. Some auction sites promote the competition aspect of online bidding. If not properly taught, children can get caught up in a bidding war and not realize how expensive an item has become. Many of these online auctions are teaching consumers to win at any cost. On some rare or limited items this may be appropriate, but for most items, buying becomes the motivation, rather than satisfying the desire for a particular product. When working with these sites, bidders need to beware.

Parents should educate their children about how these businesses make money and encourage them to settle on a maximum amount to spend before engaging in a bidding war. eBay, for instance, makes money through an insertion fee (the fee for starting an auction) and a final value fee (a percentage of what the item sold for).

This money comes from the seller. The higher the final price, the more money the auction site makes.

Businesses see children as the consumers of tomorrow and spend millions of dollars to entice youngsters to their websites. For businesses, it is cheaper to spend the money online than in traditional brick-and-mortar stores because they can service more people online. It seems to be working, because the numbers show that more and more people are buying items online. This is the wave of the future. We can't stop the tide, but we can prepare ourselves and our children by studying the issues.

Digital Commerce Topics

- Having your identity stolen (especially at nonsecure sites)

- Running up credit card and other debt

- Using online sites to identify the best prices for items

Thinking about Digital Commerce

- Do I spend time researching an item before I buy it?

- Am I aware of how much I am spending online?

Talking to Your Children about Digital Commerce

- How often do you go to auction or commercial websites (such as eBay or Amazon.com) just to look at items?

- If you purchase items online, are you aware of security at the site?

Digital Commerce Keywords

- online auction policies
- online shopping
- research online before buying
- technology and identity theft

Digital Commerce Extra

Online Consumer Safety

The 2007 holiday season saw more than $20 billion in sales online, according to Enid Burns of the ClickZ Network. With online shopping increasing each year, all consumers—kids and adults—need to know how to protect themselves. Here are a few tips adapted from a British consumer confidence website.

Is the site reputable? The first rule is common sense. Why buy from someone on the Internet if you wouldn't walk into the same person's store down the block? Apply your everyday face-to-face purchasing rules to retailers you find on the Internet and you are more likely to be satisfied with your shopping experience.

Is the site you found online the best place to buy the item? Don't assume that just because someone has a website that he or she has the best selection or price. Spend some time doing research to determine the best site for the item you are looking for. Become more aware of how retail sites are promoted. The following list offers methods for locating retail sites and what to be aware of:

- **Unsolicited e-mail.** If you use unsolicited e-mail as a guide for deciding what to purchase and from whom, you could be headed for trouble. Unsolicited e-mail is an easy way for a company to contact a large number of people. If you answer the e-mail, the sender will be encouraged to send further e-mails. Many companies who use this method are "here today, gone tomorrow." They use the Internet for easy cash.

  Clicking on a link embedded in an unsolicited e-mail also leaves you vulnerable to "spoofed" websites. Spoofed websites may look exactly like a familiar and trusted site, but they often have an easy to overlook change in the URL (www.wallmart.com instead of www.walmart.com, for instance). Operators of spoofed sites typically just want your credit card information so they can use it themselves. It is also a good way of picking up viruses from harmful sites that are trying to trick you.

- **Advertisements.** Advertisements online are purchased just like those in magazines or newspapers. You might assume that the search engine or site providing the advertisement has checked the quality of the site, but that is not necessarily the case. Advertisements can be purchased by virtually anyone.

- **Search engines.** Companies at the top of search engine listings (the free listings and not the sponsored links or advertisements) are more likely to be fairly stable because it takes time to achieve this placement. Using a search engine also provides a larger selection of sites to choose from. It is still buyer beware, and it is up to the purchaser to determine the security of the site (there will be more on this topic later).

- **From another website.** If you found a website from a banner on another website, try to find out the connection. What was the site that you came from like? Was it reputable, did it recommend the site, and is it affiliated in some way? Look for real, genuine recommendations.

Is the site secure? When you arrive at a shopping website, there are some things to look for to help determine if it is reliable. Look for banners with secure shopping or association marks, but don't take it at face value just because a site says it's safe. Do your research to make sure that the site is a member of any organizations it claims. Normally this can be checked by just clicking on the banner.

Look for "https" in the URL bar. This gives a direct connection between your machine and the site server, and therefore it is more secure. It's much easier to make a web page look like a trusted page than it is to fake a URL. Also look for a lock icon on either the URL bar or in the lower right-hand corner of the browser window. This too can be an indication of a secure site (but buyers still need to do their research).

Is the business legitimate? Examine the company's contact section. Legitimate businesses are typically eager to provide multiple modes of customer interaction. Look for a real business address (not a PO Box number). If the company doesn't have a street address, how would you actually go there in person if you needed to? Also check to see if there is a dedicated customer service e-mail. Send an e-mail to see if you get answers before purchasing. Another item to check is the telephone number. If you can't get through to someone, you need to be a little suspicious. Try calling the company and asking them some questions before you make a purchase. This may save you from having a problem later.

Are there any hidden risks? You'll want to look at their stated policies. What are the policies for returns and refunds? What will happen with your private information? Neither of these are big concerns when buying face-to-face, but they are often problems online. Hidden shipping and delivery charges are an especially popular way of fooling unwary online buyers. A very low price combined with a huge handling charge may not be the deal you thought it was.

Are there any bad reviews? Finally, as mentioned before, do your research. Try looking for comments and reviews on newsgroups. Problems and negative reviews about companies can often be found there. If you are still worried, post to a newsgroup and ask other peoples' opinion.

Still not sure? If you're not sure you want to buy from a company online, find a way to make contact that is not over the Internet. Visit the shop, phone, or mail your order.

Sources

Enid Burns. (2007, December 14). *Online holiday sales peak in afternoon, sales up 19 percent.* The ClickZ Network. Retrieved January 18, 2008, from www.clickz.com/showPage.html?page=3627887

ConsumerConfidence.org.uk. (No date). *Safe online purchases.* Retrieved May 26, 2008, from www.consumerconfidence.org.uk/safe-online-purchasing.html
Used with permission.

Digital Communication

DEFINITION: *The electronic exchange of information*

When thinking about digital technologies, one of the first things that comes to mind is communication—whether using cell phones, e-mail, instant messaging, web pages, blogs, or social networking sites. Technology has certainly changed the way most of us stay in touch. Look at the way we communicated when we were children, and compare that to how children communicate today. Even 10 years ago the thought of giving a seven- or eight-year-old a cell phone was unthinkable. But now some grade school children take their own cell phones to school. Times certainly have changed.

But how are these communication methods monitored and evaluated? Parents may have a very good reason to give a seven-year-old a cell phone, but is the child taught how and when to use this piece of technology? In my youth, my parents explained to me the proper way to answer a phone. We practiced this skill over and over again. Do parents today do the same for cell phones? Have we had enough years with this communication device to know what is considered appropriate?

What about the other digital communication methods? Do your children chat online? If so, who do they talk to? Who is in their friends list? Are your kids a member of a social networking community? If so, what kind of information do they post there? These are just a few of the questions to ask yourself (and your children). Knowing the answers may provide insight into the other elements as well. The digital communication element overlaps with a number of other elements, including digital access, digital etiquette, digital rights and responsibilities, and digital security.

This element should have all parents stepping back to ask what communication technologies are being used by their children and the purpose for their use. There may be times when a particular technology may not be the best choice for the type of communication needed. There may be times when the communication itself is inappropriate.

Digital Communication Topics

- Being aware of the different digital communication methods (such as cell phones, instant messaging, and blogging)

- Monitoring children's communication using digital technologies

- Identifying when to use certain digital communication technologies

Thinking about Digital Communication

- Are there times when a specific digital communication device may not be the best for the occasion?

- Am I being a good role model in my use of digital communication technology?

Talking to Your Children about Digital Communication

- If your child is using instant messaging (IM), do you know who they talk to? How many online "friends" do they have? How well do they know them?

- How many of your children's friends are using digital communication tools on a regular basis? Do they use them once a month, once a week, or daily?

Digital Communication Keywords

- appropriate e-mail use

- cell phone etiquette

- text messaging issues

- Web 2.0 communication tools

Digital Communication Extra

Instant Messaging Lingo

Parents with children who are instant messaging online or texting on their cell phones are aware that there is a whole other language out there. Some of the new words are used for speed and efficiency. Others are code for when adults might be around. For those who have not yet learned about this shorthand lingo, here is a brief list of the more popular abbreviations.

ASL: Age/sex/location

BRB: Be right back

CD9: Code 9 (means parents are around)

D8: Date

DIKU?: Do I know you?

F2F: Face-to-face

GR8: Great

H8: Hate

KPC: Keep parents clueless

L8R: Later

LOL: Laughing out loud or laugh out loud

MOS: Mom over shoulder

PAW: Parents are watching

PIR: Parent(s) in room

POS: Parent(s) over shoulder

PRON or pr0n: Intentional misspelling of porn

SOB: Stressed out big-time

TTFN: Ta ta for now

TTYL, TTUL, T2UL, or T2YL: Talk to you later

UOK: [Are] you OK?

Digital Literacy

DEFINITION: *The capability to use digital technology and knowing when and how to use it*

When you first look at the element of digital literacy, it may appear to be a topic that should be addressed only in schools. The concepts of teaching and learning do have much to do with schools, but as much (or more) to do with you. Parents are where teaching and learning begin. From the day we are born (and some argue even before), parents are the ones who initiate the teaching process. Children often emulate the actions and activities of their parents. Kids are often eager and willing to learn new technologies, and sometimes they are one step ahead. Consequently, parents need to make a concerted effort to learn new technologies—not just the nuts and bolts of practical use, but the methods and means of appropriate use. Parents should be the first stop for kids who have questions about technology use.

Digital literacy includes taking the time to think about issues that might come about with the use of technology. Appendix B looks at four of the most popular technologies currently being purchased for children (MP3 players, gaming systems, computers, and cell phones) and provides starting points for discussion. I hope these ideas trigger additional thinking and solutions for parents concerned about these technologies.

Digital literacy needs to be addressed in the home but also in partnership with schools. First, there needs to be a determination of what children should know about technology and what they are being taught. At school, are children learning specific computer programs (such as Microsoft PowerPoint) or are they learning technology concepts? Are they learning skills that apply just to today or to their entire lives? Second, schools and parents need to work together so that what is taught in one place does not contradict what is taught in the other. This is why adopting a program of digital citizenship in schools is important—so that parents and educators can work together.

Digital Literacy Topics

- Learning about the technology before using it

- Leading by example when using technology

- Understanding the connection between technology and education

Thinking about Digital Literacy

- Do I have a good grasp on what it means to be literate in a digital society?

- What are the basic skills that all technology users need to be effective?

Talking to Your Children about Digital Literacy

- How do your children learn about using new technologies?

- How can parents and children work together to understand how technologies work and how to use them appropriately?

Digital Literacy Keywords

- online education

- technology education

- technology literacy

- understanding technology

Digital Literacy Extra

Website Evaluation

All technology users need to be literate in determining if the information on a website is accurate. Because it has become easy to post information to the web—even inaccurate or inappropriate information—parents and kids both need to know how to evaluate sites. The following ideas from Joe Landsberger, author and developer of the Study Guides and Strategies website, show what to look for.

Evaluating Website Content: Five Guidelines

1. **Authority.** Who is responsible for the page? What are the author's qualifications and associations, and can you verify them?

   Check the footer for the name of the web page author, the author's credentials and title, and the author's organizational affiliation. Is the information verifiable?

2. **Currency.** Are dates clear when the website was first created and edited?

   Check the footer for when the website was created and when it was last edited.

   Check the content for news items, indications that the site is actively maintained, and acknowledgments or responses to visitors.

3. **Coverage.** What is the focus of the site? Are there clear headings to illustrate an outline of the content? Is the navigation within the website clear?

   Check the header for a clear title and website description.

Check the content for headings and keywords.

Check the navigation to find a content outline within the website.

4. **Objectivity.** Are biases clearly stated? Are affiliations clear?

Check the content for a statement of purpose, for the type of website and potential audience, for links to information external to the website, and for graphics and cues for affiliations.

Check the header/footer and URL/domain (.gov,.com,.edu) to determine the organizational source of the website and how this reflects on the content.

5. **Accuracy.** Are sources of information and factual data listed, and available for cross-checking?

Check the content for accuracy of spelling, grammar, facts, and consistency within the website.

Check the content for a bibliographic variety of websites (external links), of electronic media (electronic databases of references), of established journals (print and online), of electronic indexes (ERIC), and of books for comparative and evaluative purposes.

Source

Joe Landsberger. (No date). *Webtruth: Evaluating website content.* Study Guides and Strategies. Retrieved August 15, 2008, from www.studygs.net/evaluate.htm
Used with permission.

Digital Etiquette

DEFINITION: *The standards of conduct expected by other digital technology users*

For generations, parents have been teaching their children to say "please," "thank you," and "excuse me" so that they could practice becoming polite members of society. Some of these niceties of etiquette have been lost by some, but many others still believe that we function better as a society when we respect one another. This is no different in our digital society. Technology users need to understand that for us all to function as digital citizens we have to be aware of others around us and how they see us.

How often do you hear loud, obnoxious cell phone ringtones at the most inopportune times? Do you hear others speaking so loudly on their cell phones that you feel a part of the conversation? Have you observed people carrying on a conversation without removing the headphones to their MP3 players? More than likely if you have seen or heard these things, your children have as well. What do you say to your children when you see this type of behavior?

Digital etiquette goes beyond cell phones and MP3 players. The idea of etiquette with technology was talked about when the Internet first appeared. Early on, the concept of *netiquette* held that Internet users were to act in a certain way while online. Early adopters of the Internet monitored other users. If people acted in a way contrary to the policies of a particular website, they were notified. Now, however, without a common code for all technology users to live by, it is difficult to determine who is behaving appropriately and who is not.

Parents need to decide early on how they want their children to act with respect to technology. Most people see technology use as a solitary activity, such as using a computer to get on the Internet. However, with the proliferation of new devices and communication methods, there are many more aspects to consider. In Chapter 4, the Cycle of Technology Use discusses the idea of reflecting on our own actions to come to a better understanding of digital citizenship. We also need to consider the norms and customs of users from around the world. Digital citizenship is important not just for one country, but for everyone who uses and interacts with digital technology.

Digital Etiquette Topics

▪ Being aware of how your actions could be interpreted by others

▪ Using mobile devices in public spaces

▪ Doing things that could be considered poor digital etiquette (for instance, TYPING MESSAGES IN ALL CAPS signifies shouting)

Thinking about Digital Etiquette

▪ Am I aware of how I use digital technology, such as cell phones, or have they become second nature?

▪ Do I notice others making mistakes when they use digital technology?

Talking to Your Children about Digital Etiquette

▪ Does the way that some people use digital technology make you uncomfortable?

▪ What happens when you see someone do something inappropriate with technology? Do other people notice? How do they react or address the situation?

Digital Etiquette Keywords

▪ acceptable use policies (AUPs)

▪ cell phone etiquette

▪ netiquette

▪ technology etiquette

Digital Etiquette Extra

Internet Etiquette

Kids need to know the proper behavior when they go online. The following guidelines are provided by TeacherVision, a popular educational website.

Netiquette

Netiquette is a term used to describe proper etiquette on the Internet. For the most part it refers to accepted practices for composing and sending e-mail, newsgroup messages, and listserv messages—and participating in chat rooms. Following are guidelines that are considered important by experienced Internet users.

Use a Subject Line. Always include a subject line in your message. The recipient will know, at a glance, what's coming and will be able to recognize the message in the future.

Use Proper Capitalization. Don't type your message in all uppercase or all lowercase letters; it makes your message difficult to read. In e-mail and chat-room messages, all capital letters indicate that someone is "shouting."

Spelling and Grammar Matter. Poorly worded, misspelled messages are hard to read, can be confusing, and make an unfavorable impression. Use correct grammar and spelling.

Use the Quote Feature in Your Replies. When replying to an e-mail message, include enough of the original message to provide the reader with context—but it is not necessary to resend the entire original message.

Limit Use of Shortcuts. To save time and typing, people tend to use shortcuts to convey emotions and commonly used phrases when communicating over the Internet. When making jokes or trying to convey emotions, some people use emoticons, symbols made out of keyboard characters. Some examples are

    :-)   smile

    :-(frown

    ;-)   wink

Common acronyms include BTW (by the way) and IMHO (in my humble opinion). While these shortcuts are harmless up to a point, encourage children to convey their feelings through their writing.

Don't Send Private Information. Never assume that your e-mail message is private, even if you send it to only one person. Others may be able to read what you write. Never send anything that you wouldn't mind reading in your local newspaper or seeing on a TV news program—with your name as the author! Likewise, don't forward a personal message that you received to others without first getting the author's consent.

Don't Be Rude or Offensive. When you communicate via computer, remember that there is a person (or many persons) who will receive your writing. Some Internet users feel a freedom to write whatever they want without regard to others' feelings. Instead, imagine the face of the person you are writing to, and don't write things you wouldn't say to that person's face. Remember: your words go out into cyberspace and can be forwarded many times—and they may come back to haunt you!

Give Credit Where It's Due. This is especially important when doing research. Most work that someone has placed on the Internet is free for you to use—but if you do use it, give the writer or creator credit.

Don't Break the Law. There are many software products available on the Internet. Many of these products are offered free of charge. Be sure the software product you are downloading is not a commercial product that has been distributed illegally. Most commercial software products have a title screen with a copyright statement.

Source

TeacherVision. (No date). *Netiquette.* Retrieved August 15, 2008, from www.teachervision.fen.com/tv/printables/netguide31_33.pdf

Digital Law

DEFINITION: *The legal rights and restrictions governing technology use*

All societies need some type of rules, policies, or laws to provide a context for how people are expected to behave to maintain order. Without laws or other guidelines, some people will take advantage of the situation and act contrary to the best interests of the group. In the early years of digital technologies (the late 1970s and 1980s), pockets of technology leaders set the guidelines on their sites that required those who used their technology to act in a certain way. On Internet sites this was called *netiquette*. Where strong leaders were not present, users were allowed to do pretty much as they wanted. Today, the numbers of sites and various digital technologies have grown so quickly that the small numbers of gatekeepers are not enough. All users need to help provide direction so that everyone uses technology appropriately.

The Internet has not only created a place for people to come together to share information, but now people can take information from others and distribute it freely. Peer-to-peer (P2P) sites, for instance, have become very popular. Often these sites take copyrighted material and provide it to anyone with access to the site. Consequently, the government has had to step in and create laws that govern these activities. The problem is that if the laws become too restrictive in one country, the people supporting the server will simply relocate to another country. If digital citizenship is to reach its full potential, it has to be embraced by all users of technology, not just those in one country.

When technologies like the Internet first appeared, if no one enforced the etiquette guidelines, there was little recourse for unsuitable behavior. It was similar to the "Wild West," with a lot of inappropriate activity and too few people to keep the peace. Now that some of these technologies have "grown up," we need rules, policies, and laws to govern ourselves. The livelihoods of some people are tied to these technologies (telecommuters, proprietors of online stores, software engineers, technology support personnel), and they need the backing from legal entities to protect their investments.

Law enforcement, however, is still catching up to the challenges presented by digital technologies. For some people, it's not happening fast enough. Others are concerned that if governmental agencies get too involved, technology will become constrained and less functional. If all users know and understand digital citizenship, there may need to be fewer laws, but as stated before, societies have laws for a reason—to protect their citizens.

Digital Law Topics

- Violating copyrights

- Slandering individuals online

Thinking about Digital Law

- Do I share copyrighted material with others (software, music, movies)?

- How would I feel if I had information posted that others used without my permission (especially if I was expecting to be paid for it)?

- Do I say things to people online that I wouldn't say to them face-to-face?

Talking to Your Children about Digital Law

- Do you go to peer-to-peer (P2P) sites? If so, do you know if the material is copyrighted?

- What is the importance of having technology laws?

Digital Law Keywords

- peer-to-peer software
- P2P
- software piracy
- technology copyright laws

Digital Law Extra

Use Illegal Music Downloading To Give Kids A Lesson On Ethics

Parents, here's a scary sign of the times: Nearly a third of youths ages 9 to 14 may be accomplices in an ongoing multibillion-dollar Internet music heist.

That's my interpretation of a survey released in late January by the NPD market research firm. According to the report, 26 percent of tweens are downloading music illegally.

They are tapping into a free file-sharing program called LimeWire, which operates as a so-called peer-to-peer network. This "P2P" technology, which allows users to download or upload music, videos and other media, has been at the center of often-confusing copyright battles in recent years. It has resulted in high-profile lawsuits by the recording industry aimed at everyone from sixth-graders to college students.

Despite the legal and educational push to combat pirating, LimeWire ranked as the second-most popular source for music file-sharing among the nearly 3,400 youngsters surveyed by NPD.

The most popular site? Not surprisingly, Apple's iTunes, which charges 99 cents per song. It was used by nearly 50 percent of the kids polled.

What's The Big Deal?

Why is it OK to download a Foo Fighters song on iTunes but wrong on LimeWire? It boils down to money: Apple, Amazon and other companies pay fees to music artists for the rights to sell their music. But no such royalty arrangement occurs when your child downloads a song for free on

LimeWire or other similar site, then burns it onto a CD for friends. The youngster is "pirating" the music without paying for it.

I found the survey troubling for a range of reasons, starting with basic ethical issues of children engaging in illegal activity. What the study also showed is many young children growing up in this digital age are unsupervised online. In fact, two-thirds of the tweens surveyed by NPD said they use the Internet without parental supervision. An additional 59 percent said they downloaded music without parental assistance.

So much for parental vigilance.

"The music industry hoped that litigation and education might encourage parents to keep better tabs on their kids' digital music activities," NPD analyst Russ Crupnick said in a statement. "But the truth is, many kids continue to share music" through sites such as LimeWire.

But why penalize children? Companies such as LimeWire are essentially encouraging illegal behavior.

True, LimeWire's website rightfully includes extensive warnings and disclaimers about safely using "P2P" software. It also notes that it does not "encourage or condone the illegal copying of copyrighted materials." The company says it has taken steps to improve downloading safety, and users can be locked out of the free site.

Still, the high school and college students I talked to about this issue said it is easy to skate around LimeWire's file-sharing checks and balances. Why do it? That's a no-brainer: The music is free, and the chances of getting caught by the copyright police are slim.

The Internet has democratized and popularized music, like so many other things. It's a wonderful feeling when you can find almost any song. For that reason, though, it's important for parents to make sure their children are supervised online, starting with keeping the computer in the family room or another area where usage can be observed.

Guide For Parents

Meanwhile, a nonprofit organization called Wired Safety (wiredsafety. org) offers online guides to parents and children on copyrighting issues and how to download music safely. Whether you have experienced young audiophiles in your house or have children just beginning to embrace the Internet music age, here is some ground to consider covering with them.

Make the pirating issue real to kids. Rather than focusing on the money motives of rock stars who want to be paid for their songs, talk about the ethics of plagiarizing a book report or copying a video.

Steer clear of free downloading sites. "If it's free, nobody has paid the artist" for the rights to the music, according to Wired Safety. The Recording Industry Association of America has a list of pay-to-download music sites at riaa.com.

Talk about the lack of product quality on "P2P" services. According to Wired Safety, many songs are contaminated with viruses, and others are low-quality copies of the actual recording. That claim was confirmed by the students I interviewed.

Finally, there's a money lesson to this music monitoring. If your youngster is looking to add songs to his playlist, some comparison shopping is in order. With any number of music downloading sites to choose from, shoppers may find some variation in price and quality—and it's all perfectly legal behavior.

Source

The Tampa Tribune. (2008, February 24). *Use illegal music downloading to give kids a lesson on ethics.* Retrieved from www2.tbo.com/content/2008/feb/24/bz-use-illegal-music-downloading-to-give-kids-a-le/

Digital Rights and Responsibilities

DEFINITION: *The privileges and freedoms extended to all digital technology users, and the behavioral expectations that come with them*

Certain rights are given to all members in a free democratic society. But to earn those rights the society asks that the individual also take on responsibilities. In other words, if you are to receive something from the group, you must provide to the group as well. This is the same in a digital society. To gain rights as a digital citizen you must behave in a certain way.

Unlike digital law, this element asks users to act in a certain way not because someone says so or because you may be punished if you don't, but because it is the correct thing to do as a citizen. This element is similar to digital etiquette in that you need to look at the larger good rather than just what you might get out of a given situation.

For parents it may be hard to find a balance between protecting their children and ensuring their children's rights. Some parents use RFID (radio-frequency identification) to track their children. Others use GPS (Global Positioning System) to track them, which is available in some cell phones. For older kids, a device can be placed in a car that tracks exactly where the car has been. Just like many schools, parents are placing web-filtering devices on their home computers to block objectionable sites. Using these devices is well within the rights of parents to protect their children, but are they teaching children to be responsible technology users?

Cyberbullying is another issue that has come about with the growth of technology use. Bullying used to be limited to the neighborhood or schoolyard. Now with blogs, texting, and social networking sites, it is harder for children to get away from bullies, and more difficult to identify them. Cyberbullies can remain virtually anonymous. As a part of being a digital citizen, it is important for children to inform their parents or other responsible adults about cyberbullying.

Discussing digital rights and responsibilities provides parents with an opportunity to let their children know that using technology is not just about buying new toys, but about truly understanding appropriate and inappropriate behavior. Technology use should be seen as a privilege. If people want to have the right to use technology, shouldn't they show that they are ready to use it? We do the same for driving. We ask that those who want to drive to show some level of competence. What makes technology so different?

Digital Rights and Responsibilities Topics

- Working with others to keep technology safe

- Understanding that digital citizens have certain responsibilities to others (such as kids informing a responsible adult when they see inappropriate technology use)

Thinking about Digital Rights and Responsibilities

- What do I need to learn before I use a digital technology?

- How can I help others to be good digital citizens?

Talking to Your Children about Digital Rights and Responsibilities

- What would you do if someone was chatting online about doing harm to others?

- When should you ask others for permission to use their material posted on the Internet and when is it OK to just take information for your own use?

Digital Rights and Responsibilities Keywords

- acceptable use policies (AUPs)

- responsible behavior online

Digital Rights and Responsibilities Extra

Instant Messaging Guidelines

One of the more popular ways for communication among teens and tweens is instant messaging. Most parents don't use this form of communication in their daily lives, so they may be unfamiliar with the issues associated with it. Media Awareness Network has provided some guidelines to help parents understand this technology.

Instant Messaging

Instant messaging (IM) is a form of Internet communication that combines the live nature of chat with the personal contact of e-mail.

Because you create your own list of people to talk with, instant messaging can be a safe alternative to chat rooms.

Some of the benefits of IM include:

- Talking in real time with family and friends.

- A much safer environment than chat rooms since you have only people you know on your list.

- For kids who are shy or socially ill at ease, IM can be a wonderful communications tool.

However, there are drawbacks to instant messaging:

- If kids aren't careful during the sign-up process, anyone will be able to contact them.

- Most IM software allows users to create a personal profile of themselves, with information such as name, age, e-mail address, home address, phone number, school, and hobbies. This information is then made available to any IM user on the Internet.

- Some IM programs offer users the option of joining in chat rooms with strangers.

- IM can encourage negative interaction if kids use it for gossiping and bullying.

- Kids can receive pornographic "spam" through their instant messaging program.

Safety Guidelines for Instant Messaging

Protect your kids' privacy during the registration process. When your kids register for instant messaging software, sit with them and make sure that their authorization is required before anyone adds them to an IM list. As well, discourage them from filling out the "personal profile" that some programs ask users for—this information is made available to other users, so young people should never use this option.

Help your kids create their own user list. Know who's on your kids' IM lists and what lists their names are on. Kids should only approve people for their IM lists if they know them in the "real world." Check your child's list regularly to make sure that strangers haven't been added.

Make sure the IM software they use doesn't offer access to chat rooms. Many IM programs offer access to chat rooms where users can talk to strangers. One popular program offers a link to chat rooms right on the opening screen—even if users opted out of the chat option when they registered. To avoid this problem, check your IM program carefully to make sure you can block access to chat rooms, and make sure your kids know that they're off limits.

Teach kids never to share their IM user names and passwords with others, online or in the nonvirtual world. Kids often share their IM passwords with friends, which can easily lead to account misuse.

Remind your kids to choose passwords that can't easily be guessed by others. Random combinations of letters and numbers offer the best protection against password theft.

Report pornographic junk mail to the instant messaging service provider. Even if your child's IM program has been configured to accept messages only from people on the contact list, she or he may still receive "spam," or junk mail—even pornographic spam. Use the "Ignore" function to block that sender in future, and report the spam to the service provider. Because this is a frequent problem with some IM programs, it's not recommended that young children use instant messaging.

Disable any file-sharing options. Most IM programs offer a file-sharing option that allows users to download files to your computer's hard drive. However, serious viruses can be sent to your computer this way. If your child wants to be able to receive files from friends, make sure that the file-sharing settings are configured so that you have to give your permission before a file can be downloaded to your computer.

Source

Media Awareness Network. (2008). *Instant messaging.* Retrieved July 28, 2008, from www.media-awareness.ca/english/parents/Internet/safe_passage_parents/messaging_safety_p.cfm
Used with permission.

Digital Health and Wellness

DEFINITION: *The elements of physical and psychological well-being related to digital technology use*

The concept of digital health and wellness originally focused on the physical aspects of technology use. With the changes that have occurred over the years, this element has grown to encompass many more ideas. Today, more than ever, the need to be aware of health issues is important.

When computer technology first became widespread, articles were written on associated health problems, such as carpal tunnel syndrome (or other repetitive stress injuries), eyestrain, and back pain (from poorly designed computer tables and chairs). Early computer users often used folding tables and chairs for equipment and seating, which led to a myriad of problems. As people became aware of the health concerns, ergonomic furniture and equipment began to develop and has since become a booming business. And sitting at a computer isn't the only concern. Some research has centered on the relationship between the use of cell phones and some forms of cancer. While there is still no conclusive evidence of a relationship, and the risk may be small, parents may wish to limit their children's cell phone use to essential calls (kids could use landlines for other conversations).

Technology is the constant companion for some people, because of their work or their hobbies. Some of us can't leave our cell phones at home without feeling lost. Some of us check our e-mail when we are on vacation. Some of us have difficulty being away from technology altogether. For these people, technology may be causing not only physical harm but psychological harm as well. Studies have found that some people are so dependent on technology that it is diagnosed as an addiction. When technology is taken away from these people, many experience the same reaction as an alcoholic going through withdrawal. Moderation is the answer.

For children, parents need to balance the positive aspects of the technology with the potential health risks, make sure that kids have the proper equipment, and aren't spending too much time online or with their gadgets. It helps to toss in nontechnology activities from time to time. Parents need to be good role models as well.

Digital Health and Wellness Topics

- Medical problems associated with technology use, such as repetitive stress injuries, eyestrain, and back problems

- Addiction to technology use

Thinking about Digital Health and Wellness

- Do I have proper posture when I use technology?

- Do I monitor how much time I spend using technology?

Talking to Your Children about Digital Health and Wellness

- When using technology do you use tables and chairs that are at the right height?

- How much time is too much time when using technology? Keep a chart of when you use technology in a three-day time frame and see.

Digital Health and Wellness Keywords

- cell phone cancer

- cell phone health concerns

- computer ergonomics

- health concerns with video gaming systems

- technology addiction

Digital Health and Wellness Extra

Computers and Ergonomics

SafeComputingTips.com provides advice to help people be more comfortable and productive while using their computers. One of the many articles at this website discusses ergonomics and children. The following information is adapted from that article.

In the world of technology, child ergonomics are often overlooked. However, children's use of the computer has increased dramatically over the last two decades. Kids and their parents need to pay attention to child ergonomics because children usually are working on equipment that is not made for them.

Children who use computers and other technology inappropriately can end up with eyestrain, carpal tunnel, and back problems. No matter how old a child is, preventing computer-related issues is much easier to accomplish than coping with health issues over a lifetime. Children's computer work areas should be designed with ergonomics in mind, which can teach kids good habits that will be with them for life.

SafeComputingTips.com offers the following advice.

Child Ergonomics Tips

- Position the monitor's screen at or below the child's eye level. Take the monitor off its base or have the child sit on phone books to reach the desired height.

- Because most office chairs are too big for children, use a back cushion, pillow, or rolled-up towel for back support.

- Children should place their feet on a box or footstool for comfort. Feet dangling over the chair's edge can impede circulation.

- If children and adults in your home share the same computer workstation, make certain that the workstation can be modified for each child's use.

- Wrists should be held in a neutral position while typing—not angled up or down. The mouse surface should be close to the keyboard so your child doesn't have to reach or hold the arm away from the body.

- The child's knees should be positioned at an approximate 90- to 120-degree angle. Feet can be placed on a foot rest, box, stool, or similar object.

- Reduce eyestrain by making sure there is adequate lighting and that there is no glare on the monitor screen. Use an antiglare screen if necessary.

- Limit your child's time at the computer and make sure he or she takes periodic stretch breaks during computing time.

- Your child's muscles need adequate hydration to work properly and avoid injury. Encourage your child to drink four 8-ounce glasses of water a day. Carbonated beverages, juices, and other sweet drinks are not a substitute.

Source

SafeComputingTips.com. (No date). *Child ergonomics.* Retrieved May 27, 2008, from http://safecomputingtips.com/child-ergonomics.html

Digital Security

DEFINITION: *The precautions that all technology users must take to guarantee their personal safety and the security of their network*

One of the technology topics that is least considered is the one that can cause the most problems. Most people assume that all new technology has some sort of built-in security or they just don't think about it at all. As technologies such as cell phones and MP3 players become more sophisticated, the possibility of that technology becoming infected or worse—taken over by a virus or other malicious software—becomes more real.

Most computer users know what viruses are—programs that arrive on a computer without the user's knowledge and that use up the available memory or cause other damage. However, technology users may not think about keeping their virus protection programs up-to-date, configuring firewall protection, or encrypting wireless routers for maximum protection (or they may not know how). Many don't know if they have the software or hardware they need to protect their data. Users are storing more of their personal information on their home computers. This information, if compromised, could lead to identity theft. Children need to know that the protection is there to prevent unwanted intrusion into the household information.

People may believe the cost of security software packages to be too expensive or that the time and effort to set them up is too large a burden. If you have ever spoken to people whose hard drive crashed or who had their data destroyed because of a virus or hardware failure, you can understand the stress involved. Today people bank, shop, and work on their computers. Without protection and proper backups, valuable information can be gone forever. Technology users need to determine what the potential loss of all their data would mean. Consider also that if you are not protected against viruses, you might spread them to others, potentially damaging their data through your negligence.

The newest concerns are spyware and adware. Spyware collects information about users through their Internet connections, such as the websites they go to.

This can be used for advertising purposes. Some spyware, however, compiles e-mail addresses, passwords, and credit card numbers as well. Adware is a kind of spyware that gathers information about the user's browsing preferences in order to show advertisements in the browser window specifically geared to that user.

Most technology users feel secure with the virus protection they have, but these programs rarely protect against spyware and adware. Like some viruses, spyware and adware can provide information to someone else about you and your family. Some of the information can be fairly benign, such as the sites that you and your family like to visit, but other information could be much more detrimental. Security includes having locks on your doors, but it also means securing your technology. The thieves of tomorrow will try to get into your digital doors as well as your physical ones. Antispyware and antiadware programs are available. Talk to an information technology professional to determine the program that would be most appropriate for your needs.

Digital Security Topics

- Having the proper protection for computers and other technologies

- Making sure that the protection is updated regularly

Thinking about Digital Security

- Do I have enough protection to keep intruders out of my system (or at least make it more difficult to get in)?

- Am I careful about the information I share on the Internet?

Talking to Your Children about Digital Security

- Do you tell others personal information about yourself when online?

- Do you know what viruses, spyware, and adware are? What can you do to protect yourself?

Digital Security Keywords

- adware
- computer virus
- data backup
- firewall

- spyware
- technology disaster protection
- technology protection

Digital Security Extra

Protect Your Home Computer

Most parents do not have the resources to contact a technology professional to help them keep their computer running well. Here are a few tips to protect your home computer, compiled by the Norwood School in Bethesda, Maryland (an independent elementary and middle school).

Top Tips for Computer Protection at Home

1. Buy an antivirus program, and make sure it automatically stays up-to-date. Run virus checks regularly, either automatically or manually.

2. Keep children safe online. Understand instant messaging. Do not let your children play games online with strangers. Talk to your children about guidelines for online safety, and adopt rules for Internet use.

3. Install a firewall to protect your systems from hackers. Cable or DSL modem providers often bundle their service with a firewall. Make sure your provider does. Windows XP has a built-in firewall. Make sure it is enabled.

4. Run Windows Update regularly to download and install critical updates (which are free from Microsoft). This service from the Microsoft website will automatically update your computer with security patches.

5. Download and install a spyware protection program such as Ad-Aware (free). This program monitors your computer for programs that compromise privacy.

6. Download and install a pop-up blocker such as the Google Toolbar (free), which will stop annoying pop-up windows.

7. Understand e-mail spam and use spam filtering from your provider. Do not open suspicious e-mail attachments. Delete the e-mail, and then empty the Deleted Items folder.

8. Use Internet filtering/blocking software such as AOL's Parental Controls or CyberPatrol to block inappropriate sites and limit children's computer usage time.

9. Maintain your privacy. Identity theft, child safety, and credit card fraud are just a few of the privacy concerns facing consumers online today. Your best defense is a good offense. By using some basic precautions, you can reduce the odds of being a victim.

10. Be aware of "phishing." Never give out your information online in response to an e-mail. Likewise, never give out your information over the phone.

Source

Norwood School. (No date). *Top tips for computer protection at home.* Retrieved May 27, 2008, from http://library.norwoodschool.org/ Help_FAQs/home_computing/top_tips_protection.htm

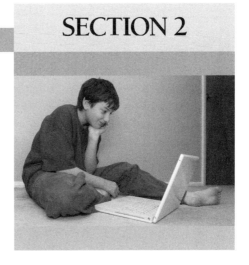

Bringing
Digital Citizenship
into the Home

Education is not the filling of a pail, but the lighting of a fire.

—W. B. Yeats

As Yeats suggests, teaching isn't all about providing information, but about sparking a passion for learning. In digital citizenship, this means not just becoming informed about the nine elements and accompanying issues, but developing enthusiasm for facing the challenges of the Digital Age and excitement for creating a skillful and responsible digital society. For kids, we want this passion to extend to caring about the digital community and doing the right thing.

Once you have some idea of the technology issues surrounding our children, you may feel either more at ease or more stressed out thinking about what to do next. But whether you're more comfortable or more concerned, you may have already realized that being made aware of problems isn't enough. We are not about to change our children's attitudes or behavior by simply pointing out the issues. We need to show them a new way of understanding technology and its appropriate use so that they can use it now and apply it to new technologies in the future.

The chapters in this section will guide you toward that new way of understanding. Chapter 3 helps you decide where to start on this journey with your children. Chapter 4 provides a process for working with new technologies that inspires self-awareness and promotes responsible behavior. Chapter 5 contains questionnaires to help you gauge your children's knowledge. All provide practical, concrete ideas for working with your kids. Together, you can kindle the flame and build a better digital society.

CHAPTER 3

Choosing an
Area of Focus

Some parents are concerned that simply having Internet access in their home practically ensures issues with what their children do online. They may have heard about online predators or identity theft. These risks may have prompted some parents to keep technology away from their children, but ignoring technology won't make the problems go away. Children will find access—at school, at a friend's house, at the library, and of course once they're out on their own. This is why parents need to step up and teach their children digital citizenship. Being able to operate technology appropriately is a critical skill that children will need as they grow. Just like knowing the rules of the road is important for drivers, knowing the responsibilities for the information highway is important for computer users.

You may be afraid to allow your children to use something you don't understand. Or you may know about the issues but aren't sure what to do. Maybe you're in digital denial and have simply chosen not to think about it. However, in order to help your children, you do have to understand, make choices, and think about it.

To help you see the relationships among the various elements of digital citizenship, I have divided them into three categories: Focus for Parents, Focus for Home and School, and Focus for Home and Community (see Categories of digital citizenship figure). Each of these focus areas needs to be discussed with your children, but two require consultation with other people as well. The Focus for Parents category includes the elements of digital commerce, digital law, and digital health and wellness. These elements tend to coincide with situations that arise with children in the home. The Focus for Home and School category includes the elements of digital literacy, digital etiquette, and digital security. Discuss these elements with school personnel, such as teachers, administrators, members of the PTA, and school board officials. Finally, the Focus for Home and Community category includes the elements of digital access, digital communication, and digital rights and responsibilities. Talk about these elements with members of your community.

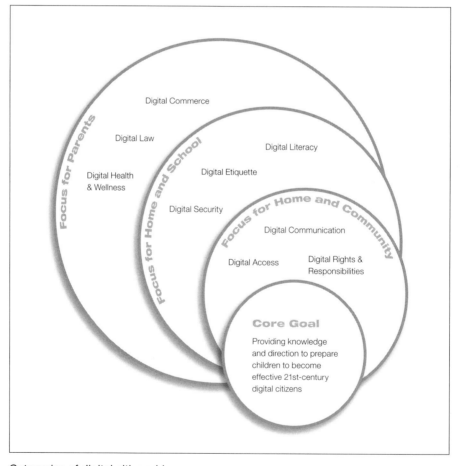

Categories of digital citizenship

Digital citizenship is so vast in scope that parents may initially feel overwhelmed and not know where to start. These three categories provide a basic outline and allow you to choose the areas that are the most important to you. Remember that topics within the nine elements do overlap. This means that topics in each of the focus areas will also overlap.

How do you decide what to work on first? What is most important to you and your family members will depend on your children. If your kids are experiencing eyestrain or are buying things online, you might want to start with Focus for Parents. If you're concerned about protection from viruses, you could start with the Focus for Home and School. If your home has been inundated with communication technology (cell phones, text messaging, instant messaging, e-mail), make the Focus on Home and Community a priority. You will need to base these decisions on your household and circumstances.

Be careful when choosing a focus area for digital citizenship. Topics that appear less important to you now still need to be understood. Eventually you should have a grasp of all the elements because new technologies may appear that put a whole new perspective on what was a nonissue for your household. For instance, when text messaging was added to cell phones, many parents did not see the significance until their children began generating high text-messaging bills. It's also important to remember the greater ramifications for technology use. If you are concerned about the way your kids use technology in the home, keep in mind that similar activities could be happening at school or out in the community.

One way to broaden the discussion is with the Family Contract for Digital Citizenship in Appendix C, which lays out some simple understandings between you and your children. The contract has a Kid's Pledge and a Parent's Pledge. Both include concepts from all nine elements. After you and your children work through this document, you will be able to communicate about each of the nine elements, even if your primary focus is only on three.

As parents, it is your responsibility to determine how you want your children to act within your home. But it is also your responsibility to provide guidance for what your children do when they are at school or in the community. Different realms of society have different rules when it comes to technology use (many for very good reasons), and children, as well as adults, need to know how to act when they cross the boundary into a different realm. For example, many schools have acceptable use policies (AUPs) to help protect the children and technology within the school and district. Parents need to work with school and community leaders to determine the best course for teaching appropriate use in their schools and community.

Technology is a very complex concept and one that is often difficult to understand. By using these categories it is hoped that parents will be able to recognize the issues of inappropriate technology use all around us and to determine what needs to be done. It also helps to realize that there is much we do not know and much we have left to learn.

Cycle of
Technology Use

As parents, we try to teach our children how to be good citizens of our country, what their rights are as well as their responsibilities as members of this society. It's just as important that children learn how to become good digital citizens in our new digital society.

The challenges we face every day are increasing. With all the pressures of today's society, it can be difficult to know how to talk to our children and what we should talk about. If parents are already uncomfortable with their digital knowledge, it can be doubly problematic. This is why it is important to have knowledge of the nine elements of digital citizenship and the issues that accompany them.

It's also important to find a way to approach a new technology, to understand what it does, how to use it appropriately, and what problems could arise from its use. We also need to develop a sense of self-awareness around technology and to reflect on how we use it. Children are typically more than willing to try out a new technology, but their willingness may surpass their understanding. It's our job as parents to put on the brakes, slow things down, and help our kids think about the new technology and its appropriate use.

I've created a four-stage reflection model to help children think about how they use technology—not just at home, but at school, out in the community, and with their friends. Called the Cycle of Technology Use, this model is to be referred to each time a child uses a new technology. As children become more aware of their actions, going through each stage will become a mental habit, one that promotes appropriate technology use throughout their lives.

The four stages are (see Cycle of Technology Use figure):

1. Awareness

2. Guided practice

3. Modeling and demonstration

4. Feedback and analysis

Review the model, and then discuss the four stages with your children. It may take time to feel comfortable with the Cycle of Technology Use, but understanding it will provide benefits in the long term. As you go through these stages with your children, always remember that nobody is perfect. Even those who use technology for a job sometimes forget some of the basics.

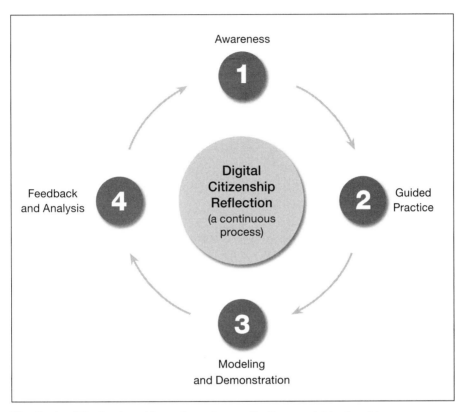

The Cycle of Technology Use, a four-stage reflection model for teaching
digital citizenship

Stage 1: Awareness

Awareness means helping your children (and yourself) become technologically literate. The awareness stage, however, goes beyond just basic knowledge of hardware and software. Children (and their parents) need to understand the *appropriate use* of digital technologies. Encourage your children to ask themselves:

- Do I have a good understanding of how a particular technology works and how using this technology can affect me as well as others?

- Have I learned about the potential problems or issues related to using this technology?

- How can I use this technology in a way that it is acceptable to my parents and friends?

Awareness Activities

Before acquiring a new technology, sit down and talk with your children about the issues that might occur. For example, before purchasing a particular cell phone for your children, find out if it has texting capability. If it does, talk with your children about the costs associated with this feature.

Before getting a new technology, establish boundaries with your children for using the technology. Explain that if a child breaks the rules, there will be consequences. To make it more meaningful, ask your kids to help come up with the rules and consequences.

Have an open discussion with other parents about technology issues. For example, before purchasing a gaming system (PlayStation, Xbox, Wii), find out if the system can connect to the Internet. If it can, discuss with other parents any issues that might arise from that feature.

Stage 2: Guided Practice

Following instruction in awareness, parents should provide children with opportunities to use the technology under their guidance and help them to recognize and demonstrate appropriate use. Children need to have an opportunity to learn the skills in a safe environment. Create an atmosphere where exploration and risk-taking are promoted. The home needs to be a place where children can investigate the technologies they use every day, including instant messaging (IM), handheld computers, and cell phones.

Children need to practice digital citizenship skills while the parent acts as a guide. Without guided practice, inappropriate use of technology can occur without children even being aware of it. During this period, children will need your support when mistakes are made.

Ask your children to reflect on the following questions:

- When I learn about a new technology, do people explain all the steps required, or do they assume that I already know how to use the technology and skip important information?

- Am I asked to demonstrate appropriate technology use to my parents (or another responsible adult), or do they take it for granted that I know the correct method?

- Do I have regular conversations with a parent or other adult on what is considered a misuse or abuse of technology?

- How do I best learn about appropriate technology use: from adults or from other sources (such as the Internet, friends, TV, or movies)?

Guided Practice Activities

Have your child think about a situation where people use cell phones in a public location, like a movie theater or a restaurant. Set up a scenario in this location where cell phone conversations are conducted in a loud and obtrusive fashion. After discussing the scenario, ask the following question: What would be the appropriate way to respond to this situation?

When your child uses technology in a manner you consider inappropriate, have the child stop immediately and discuss what should have been the correct usage and why. For example, if your child has a social networking site and has posted personal information, have the child stop and determine why this would not be a good choice.

Stage 3: Modeling and Demonstration

Parents need to be positive role models for digital citizenship so that children can follow their example. Children need to see that their parents use technology in the same way that the children are taught to use it. In other words, practice what you preach. For instance, parents with cell phones should turn them off or put them on vibrate when going to the movies or other activity. Parents should take into account copyright laws when downloading music, graphics, and other media from the Internet. Kids need to see numerous examples of appropriate technology use to gain a thorough understanding of digital citizenship. Parents should model appropriate technology use on a regular basis.

Children should be led to an understanding of cause and effect with regard to technology use. All forms of technology use, misuse, and abuse have consequences. Have your children consider the following questions:

- Do others provide good examples of how to use new technology, or do I just learn it on my own?

- Have I seen, read, or heard of situations regarding inappropriate technology use? What were the consequences?

- My friends use a certain technology one way, but my parents have shown a different behavior. Are they both appropriate? How should I use that technology?

Modeling and Demonstration Activities

Discuss with your children what is considered technology misuse and abuse at school. A school AUP (acceptable use policy) can be a great resource for this activity. Go through the AUP and ask your children how they would act in several school-related examples. Talk about how the rules may be the same or different at home. Ask your children the following questions:

- What are the different categories of technology use, misuse, and abuse at school?

- What are some examples of appropriate or inappropriate technology use at school? Why are they considered appropriate or inappropriate?

- Should we follow the same rules for technology use at home? Why or why not?

If parents make a lapse in judgment when using technology, such as forgetting to turn their cell phone to vibrate, they can discuss how they too can become better at using technology appropriately.

Stage 4: Feedback and Analysis

The home should be a place where children and their parents can discuss their use of technology to determine how they can use it more appropriately. Create an atmosphere where kids can ask questions. Encourage kids to analyze and explore why they should use technologies in a certain way. Provide feedback that will help children find ways to avoid or mitigate problems that may arise from inappropriate technology use.

It can be difficult to "go back" and think about one's actions after they occur, but self-reflection is a necessary part of the process. Without the opportunity to reconsider one's actions, inappropriate behavior will tend to be repeated.

Children need to reflect on their actions and ask themselves:

- Am I satisfied with my decision? Why or why not?

- Am I satisfied with the outcome of the situation? Why or why not?

- Did my behavior have a positive or negative effect on others? Why?

- Did I go back and evaluate how I used the technology later?

- Did I think about possible alternatives of how to use the technology?

Feedback and Analysis Activities

Make sure that your children understand the need for self-reflection on the use of technology. One possibility for parents is to ask children to keep a log of their technology use. Set up a time each week to talk about their usage.

After working with your children on using technology appropriately, you need to come to an understanding that if certain rules are broken (that have been taught, explained, and demonstrated), consequences will be enforced (such as taking away the technology or curtailing its use). If a child breaks a rule, ask for an explanation for the behavior.

Encouraging Digital Citizenship

Digital citizenship should become a priority in the home. When you integrate digital citizenship into your household, it emphasizes the importance of the topic and underscores the message that using technology is a privilege and not a right. Children need to see that being a good citizen is just as important in the digital world as in their community. That message should be reinforced by the family. To help establish appropriate technology use, go through the four-stage Cycle of Technology Use as often as needed. It isn't an easy process, especially at first, but once your kids go through it a few times and see the benefits, the process will become easier.

Waiting to talk about digital citizenship until children are in their teens may be too late. Digital citizenship should be discussed as soon as children begin using digital technologies. The time to start teaching digital citizenship is now.

Technology misuse and abuse are widespread and can be found everywhere in our communities. We want to prepare our children to be productive members of society, and being a good digital citizen is part of that equation. Although rules and policies are important, they are not enough. Children must learn what is appropriate and inappropriate—an understanding that comes through discussion and dialogue, not just by following a set of rules. You can't expect to eliminate all mistakes, but you can lessen them by following this process.

The next time you hear a cell phone ring in a movie theater or at a wedding, ask yourself if that person is a responsible digital citizen or yet another example of someone who has not yet learned the importance of digital citizenship. Education (in many forms) is crucial to achieving digital citizenship in the 21st century.

CHAPTER 5

Finding Out
What Your Kids Know

Some people assume that because children grow up with technology around them, they instantly know everything about technology. This is simply not the case. A large number of children struggle with the basics of technology, such as using a word processor or a cell phone. The same is true for digital citizenship. Just because children grow up around technology doesn't mean they understand its appropriate use. The good news is, just as technology skills can be taught, digital citizenship can be taught.

In 2001, Marc Prensky wrote *Digital Natives, Digital Immigrants*. He stated that those who grow up around technology are digital natives, and the rest of us are simply immigrants trying to learn the "language" of technology. Given the speed of changing technology, I would assert that everyone is an immigrant at some time, even young technology users. Everyone is constantly learning the new "language" of technology as one type of equipment replaces another.

The "language" of technology and the speed of change extend to digital citizenship as well. We all need to have the same "vocabulary" of appropriate technology use so that we can work, play, and learn together. Without this ability to understand one another, problems will inevitably arise. And because new technologies appear every day, we are all constantly reinventing ourselves as digital citizens.

Adults may not want to subject themselves to "language" lessons. However, we cannot teach our children how to use the "language" correctly if we don't speak it ourselves. Is it difficult to keep up with the constant changes in technology and the appropriate behavior for its use? Certainly. But if we don't keep pace and teach our children, who will?

The truth is, young people are more likely to learn from one another. It is not unusual for one child to explain to another how a task was accomplished (in a computer game, for instance). Misinformation is passed on just as readily as correct information, but children are more likely to assume information is correct when they hear it from another child. This is how problem behaviors are perpetuated. Consequently, it's in the best interests of parents to dig in, learn about digital citizenship, and stay up-to-date so they can pass on the correct information to their kids.

Once you've learned a few things about digital citizenship yourself, a good place to start with your children is to find out what they already know. The following pages contain two quizzes on digital citizenship. The first is geared toward younger children (ages 7–11), and the second toward older kids (ages 12–17). The answers that the children select will provide some idea of their knowledge on the topic.

For those who have a strong understanding of the basic information, the quiz will solidify that knowledge and provide a foundation for further study. For those who are not as proficient, the quiz will help pinpoint areas where more information is needed.

Source

Marc Prensky. (2001). Digital natives, digital immigrants. *On the Horizon, 9*(5), 10–15.

Quiz for Younger Children (Ages 7–11)

Digital Manners (Etiquette)

1. Having your cell phone turned on during dinner with your family is:

   a. a bad idea because it might interrupt your family.

   b. a good idea for keeping in touch with friends.

   c. no big deal because everyone else does it.

   d. your choice, one that doesn't affect anyone else.

Digital Messages (Communication)

2. When writing on a blog, should you share personal information (address, phone number, birthday)?

   a. Sure. A blog is like a diary, so personal information is important.

   b. It doesn't matter. Only my friends read my blog.

   c. No. A blog can be open to people you may not want having that information.

   d. Sure, as long as I don't use my name.

Digital Learning (Literacy)

3. When learning about technology, it is important for you to know:

   a. the rules for using technology.

   b. how to work with others when using the technology.

   c. how different technologies are used.

   d. all of the above.

Digital Inclusion (Access)

4. Children with disabilities (those who aren't able to see, hear, or walk):

   a. can't use technology.

   b. should have the same opportunities as others to use technology.

   c. are not able to understand and learn about technology.

   d. have no reason to use technology.

Digital Business (Commerce)

5. If your parents allow you to buy things on the Internet, you should protect yourself by:

   a. doing nothing, because all Internet sites are safe and protected.

   b. doing nothing, because your friends do it and that makes it OK.

   c. not telling anyone that you are buying things from the Internet.

   d. not forgetting to see if the site is safe and secure before buying something.

Digital Trust (Law)

6. When using graphics and text from the Internet, you should:

   a. use as many as possible.

   b. give the information to as many people as possible.

   c. give credit to the author of the information.

   d. stop, because you should never use anything from the Internet.

Digital Privileges (Rights and Responsibilities)

7. When using a new technology at home, you should:

   a. do whatever you want because no one ever checks.

   b. talk to your parents about what is appropriate.

   c. not ask permission because your parents always say no.

   d. ask your friends because they know about technology.

Digital Protection (Health and Wellness)

8. How you work with technology (such as sitting at a desk, lying on the floor, or resting on the sofa):

    a. doesn't matter as long as you are comfortable.

    b. depends on where you are.

    c. isn't something that you need to be concerned about.

    d. is important because poor posture can cause physical problems later in life.

Digital Precautions (Security)

9. When dealing with people online, giving personal information is:

    a. OK as long those people live far away.

    b. never a good idea, no matter the reason.

    c. fine as long as the people are nice.

    d. nothing to worry about.

Answer Sheet—Quiz for Younger Children

1. a Parents are allowing their children to have cell phones at increasingly younger ages, but they need to set rules for when they should be turned off or silenced. Parents and children should communicate their expectations for technology use.

2. c Blogs can be open to more users than you are aware. Some blogs can limit who can see the information, but sharing any personal information where there is public access, like the Internet, needs to be controlled. Because blogs have been explained as similar to diaries (and used as such), many users think they should share their personal information on their blogs. Blogs can be useful tools to share information, but users need to be careful what they share.

3. d Technology affords many opportunities for children to learn beyond home and school. But there must be an understanding of how to use the technologies first.

4. b Children with disabilities should have opportunities to work and learn with technology. Some children may need special technology tools to provide this opportunity (such as screen readers, special input devices, or speech-to-text converters).

5. d Purchasing goods and services online needs to be taken seriously. People can gain information about you and your family from information that you provide. Make sure the site is secure by checking it over. (For example, does it have secure access only, does it ask only questions that are appropriate for the purchase, does it have alternate ways to contact the company?)

6. c Children need to realize that when "borrowing" anything from the Internet, its use is restricted by the owner (unless stated otherwise). All content taken from the web should be cited appropriately.

7. b All users have certain rights and responsibilities when using technology. It is important to know what is appropriate and what is not appropriate before using technology.

8. d People often don't think about safe technology use habits until they hurt themselves. How you use technology today can have a big effect on how you will be able to use it in the future.

9. b It is easy to act differently online than face-to-face. Children need to make sure that private information remains private.

Quiz for Young Adults (Ages 12–17)

Digital Etiquette (the standards of conduct expected by other digital technology users)

1. When attending a concert or other public activity, the correct cell phone ringer setting is:

   a. low.

   b. vibrate.

   c. specialized ringtone.

   d. high.

2. Wearing the headphones of an MP3 player when talking to someone is:

   a. fine since I can hear both.

   b. all right if I uncover one ear.

   c. disrespectful to the other person.

   d. something everyone does.

Digital Communication (the electronic exchange of information)

3. E-mail messages should be:

   a. long and full of details.

   b. sent to as many recipients as possible.

   c. short and to the point.

   d. sent without a subject line.

4. Instant messaging (IM) is a good tool for:

   a. sharing what happened at home with friends.

   b. communicating with friends you know.

   c. talking to people you don't know.

   d. meeting people you have never met.

Digital Literacy (the capability to use digital technology and knowing when and how to use it)

5. One of the first Internet skills children should learn at home is:

   a. downloading songs and movies.

   b. finding and evaluating online resources.

   c. sharing information on social networking sites.

   d. finding and playing the latest games.

6. Determining whether a website has accurate information is:

   a. difficult and not worth the time.

   b. not necessary because everything on the web is true.

   c. impossible because there is conflicting information online.

   d. an important skill for everyone.

Digital Access (full electronic participation in society)

7. Assistive technology for people with disabilities is:

   a. necessary for some users to access information.

   b. just an additional expense.

   c. expensive relative to regular technology.

   d. limited to such a small group that it isn't important.

8. The fact that some people have access to technology and some people don't is:

   a. not a big deal because all technology is a luxury.

   b. something that can never be fixed.

   c. a concern that needs to be addressed by parents.

   d. not a priority for parents.

Digital Commerce (the buying and selling of goods online)

9. Purchasing goods and services online is:

   a. a waste of time because selling goods on the Internet is a scam.

   b. something that everyone has learned at home.

   c. not a skill to be overlooked by parents.

   d. not a skill needed by children and young adults.

10. Searching for information about products online before buying is:

   a. important if you are looking for the best price.

   b. too time consuming.

   c. a lot of work and not very informative.

   d. not helpful, because it is difficult to find products online.

Digital Law (the legal rights and restrictions governing technology use)

11. Information on the Internet is:

   a. available for people to use as they want.

   b. copyrighted and should be treated as someone else's property.

   c. easy to copy and paste so it looks like something original.

   d. unreliable and should be held suspect.

12. Sharing copyrighted musical or entertainment files online:

   a. doesn't hurt anyone because musicians and actors make enough money.

   b. is caused by greedy companies because they charge too much for CDs and DVDs.

   c. is illegal and should not be done.

   d. keeps the musician or actor popular.

Digital Rights and Responsibilities (the privileges and freedoms extended to all digital technology users, and the behavioral expectations that come with them)

13. If someone puts copyrighted material on the Internet and another person wants to use it, that person should:

    a. use it, if it is for educational use.

    b. take it and use it as he or she wants.

    c. not use the information because citing it correctly or contacting the author is too much trouble.

    d. ask permission from the author or at least cite the source.

14. If children see or hear something that concerns them online:

    a. they should ignore it and go on with their business.

    b. they should contact a responsible adult and inform them of the issue.

    c. they should tell their friends so that they can see it too.

    d. they should never talk about it because someone could get into trouble.

Digital Health and Wellness (the elements of physical and psychological well-being related to digital technology use)

15. Physical injuries related to technology use:

    a. are not a major concern.

    b. will not happen for many years, so should not be a priority.

    c. can have dramatic and painful effects on your body.

    d. rarely happen at home.

16. Furniture and chairs for technology should be:

    a. the right height and size for using that technology.

    b. any size because it doesn't matter to children.

    c. bigger than the children to allow them to stretch.

    d. soft and flexible so that children can be comfortable.

17. Children's technology use:

    a. is important for their future and should be encouraged.

    b. should be monitored to allow for a healthy lifestyle.

    c. is not important and should not be an issue for parents.

    d. is an issue only for schools and other organizations.

Digital Security (the precautions that all technology users must take to guarantee their personal safety and the security of their network)

18. When dealing with strangers, online users should:

    a. give personal information freely.

    b. be cautious about giving information.

    c. provide passwords and credit information if asked.

    d. not tell anyone about people they meet online.

19. To protect a computer from viruses, a user should:

    a. never open an e-mail message.

    b. unplug the computer from the Internet.

    c. keep up-to-date virus protection.

    d. trust the service provider to protect the computer.

20. Virus protection and firewalls are:

    a. foolproof and never need to be checked.

    b. a waste of time and money because virus attacks only happen to big businesses.

    c. effective but not necessary.

    d. a good investment, but they need to be monitored and updated regularly.

Answer Sheet—Quiz for Young Adults

1. b Vibrate is correct because it is the least distracting setting when attending an event. Many parents give their children cell phones for safety and security reasons. For that reason, you would want the cell phone turned on, but quiet. A specialized ringtone might allow you to identify your own phone, but the sound could be annoying to people attending the event. Another option would be to turn off the phone during an event.

2. c When talking to someone else you should give that person your attention. Listening to an MP3 player (even with one ear) does not provide that consideration. Think about how you would feel if someone listened to only part of what you had to say.

3. c E-mail is intended for short communication. Long and involved e-mails are often either not read or filed for later review. A descriptive subject line can alert the user about the importance and content of the e-mail.

4. b Children can use IM to talk to their friends. IM is not a place to gossip, waste time, or exclude others from the conversation. Children (and their parents) need to know who they are talking to online.

5. b Parents and children need to be able to find and evaluate websites and other online resources. Some websites appear to have good information but on closer examination it may not be what you are looking for.

6. d Being able to determine whether the information that you are reading online is true is a skill that all technology users need. With a little training almost anyone can post information online, whether it is true or not. The validity must be determined by the reader. With Web 2.0 tools it has become even easier to post information online.

7. a Some children (and adults) with disabilities need assistive technology to access digital information. Everyone should have an opportunity to access information. Many of these technologies are very cost effective.

8. c There is still a "digital divide" between those who have access to technologies and those who do not. Often basic technology needs go unfulfilled, even as prices decrease. As society becomes more technologically integrated, communities need to work with parents and public organizations to develop a plan for addressing this need.

9. c Teenagers are becoming one of the largest groups of online consumers. It is important to protect them from exploitation. The process of buying goods online needs to be taught and discussed.

10. a The Internet offers many opportunities to buy and sell goods, but the smart shopper looks around to find the best value. With the search tools that are available today, finding many different vendors is quick and easy. Looking up reviews on various products is also a cinch.

11. b According to copyright law, anything that is produced by an individual is copyrighted whether that person has gone through the legal process or not. It may be easy to copy something from the web and pass it off as original work, but this is plagiarism. Provide citations and give people credit for their work.

12. c Downloading materials without an artist's consent is stealing. Often users know that taking files from the Internet is wrong but rationalize it for a variety of reasons (such as high cost or availability).

13. d If material is copyrighted, users must give credit to the person who created it. If you are going to make a profit from a source, permission must be obtained. Copyrighted material can be used for educational purposes in some circumstances, but the rules of copyright need to be understood and followed.

14. b Children need to be taught that if they see or hear something online that makes them nervous they need to contact a responsible adult. It may seem easier to walk away from the situation, but children need to know that this could injure someone else.

15. c Repetitive stress injuries happen after extended periods of using technology incorrectly. There are long-term effects, but there are also short-term effects that include fatigue, eye problems, and sore muscles.

16. a When purchasing technology, parents need to consider how that technology will be arranged for children. Furniture that is the wrong size or not made for that purpose can make it difficult for children to use the technology. It can also lead to technology-related injuries such as repetitive stress, eyestrain, and sore muscles.

17. b Parents need to be aware of the amount of time that their children are using technology. Sitting in front of a computer or gaming system for extended periods of time can lead to an unhealthy lifestyle. Those using technology excessively can also become addicted to its use.

18. b It can be very difficult to know who you are communicating with when using digital technology. It is easy for people to disguise their identity online. Be cautious about giving out personal information such as a home address or phone number. Do not give out passwords or credit information.

19. c Protecting one's computer from viruses takes diligence on the part of the user. It is necessary to maintain virus protection. You should not open e-mails (especially attachments) from people you do not know.

20. d Virus protection, firewalls, surge protectors, and battery backups are all appropriate tools to help protect your technology investment, but purchasing them is not enough. These tools need to be monitored and updated to ensure they are working properly.

SECTION 3

Digital Citizenship
for Everyone

There is no reason anyone would want a computer in their home.

> —Ken Olson, president, chairman, and founder of Digital Equipment Corporation, 1977

How quickly things change. Technology is one of those areas where people have learned not to say the word "never." From the personal computer to cell phones, ideas about technology have changed over time as they have become a part of our everyday life.

This section is meant to broaden your understanding of digital citizenship. Chapter 6 provides a variety of facts that describe technology use in the workplace and in our greater society. Chapter 7 explores the ramifications of Web 2.0 and the advent of social networking on the Internet. Chapter 8 brings it all together and reinforces the importance of working together with your kids, your schools, and your communities.

Throughout this book I have attempted to show that everyone who uses digital technologies needs to understand digital citizenship because of the communal nature of technology use. The way we use technology often affects other people. I wrote this book to help parents prepare their children for a world full of technology. It is easier to teach people correctly the first time than to change their habits later.

Learn what your children are doing with digital technologies and what they want to do. Find out what technologies they are using with their peers. Investigate the positive and negative aspects of the technologies they are using. This book provides information and skill-building ideas, but it will not take the place of interacting with your children. We may believe that with the advance of technology, our children need less attention, but the opposite could well be true—children need as much (or more) help and guidance today as they ever did. We can help them only if we know the answers to their questions, and we will know the answers only if we study the issues.

CHAPTER 6

Help Your Children,
Help Society

The old adage "Give a man a fish and he will eat for a day; teach a man to fish and he will eat for a lifetime" applies here. If you tell your children to put away their cell phones at dinner, you will have a quiet dinner. However, if you teach your children the fundamentals of digital citizenship, such as why it is important to be considerate of others when using technology, they will be able to apply the concepts outside the home and take them on into adulthood.

What we teach our children will affect how they act and perform in school and beyond. Parents and educators need to become partners in how technology is provided and taught to children. There need to be plans in place for teaching technology skills and appropriate use in school, and these arrangements need to be carried over into the home. Some school districts are working well with parents to construct a roadmap of where children need to be with respect to technology, but sadly, in many locations that conversation has not begun. I urge parents to start this dialogue with educators. It is very important that children have a sound understanding of digital citizenship before they venture out on their own.

How important is it? When discussing the nine elements in Chapter 2, I mentioned several issues that could arise with respect to our children. This chapter provides additional examples of technology abuse that have been documented in society and in business. These examples demonstrate that the problems that are occurring at home and in education can become larger social issues and carry over into the workplace. Take in the facts, and then use the sources here and the keywords from Chapter 2 to do your own Internet research. Look for other issues that are occurring all around us. Use the information to educate yourself and your children.

This chapter is designed to help parents see how understanding digital citizenship can help their children not just at home and at school, but when they move on to the next level. As parents, it is our hope that we are preparing our children to become active, effective members of society. This should be true for our digital society as well.

Digital Access Facts

DEFINITION: *Full electronic participation in society*

Societal Incidents. Even with the decreasing costs of technology, there is still a significant difference in the amount of access that non-Hispanic white users have in relation to other ethnic groups. In a report released by the Pew Internet & American Life Project, Latinos account for 14% of the adult U.S. population. While 56% of this group goes online, 71% of non-Hispanic whites, and 60% of non-Hispanic blacks use the web.

Source

Susannah Fox and Gretchen Livingston. (2007, March 14). *Latinos online*. Pew Internet & American Life Project. Retrieved May 20, 2008, from http://pewresearch.org/pubs/429/latinos-online

Related Workplace Issues. A 2004 Commerce Department report, *A Nation Online: Entering the Broadband Age*, stated that only 1 in 7 blacks and fewer than 1 in 8 Hispanics live in a household with fast Internet service compared to 1 in 4 among white households. Lack of access could have significant impact on commerce and the availability of services.

Source

Ted Bridis. (2004, November 23). Growth of high-speed Internet disappoints some experts. *USA Today*, p. 7A. Retrieved May 20, 2008, from www.usatoday.com/tech/news/2004–11–22-high-speed-connections_x.htm

Digital Commerce Facts

DEFINITION: *The buying and selling of goods online*

Societal Incidents. Teenagers are researching and buying items over the Internet, but don't necessarily know which sites are secure or how to tell if their information is protected. According to Enid Burns, writing for the ClickZ Network, "Web adoption occurs early for college students, though web habits are still being established. Over half (53%) spend up to two hours to research prior to purchasing a product. Seventeen percent spend up to five hours."

Source

Enid Burns. (2006, February 10). *Online ads influence collegiate set.* The ClickZ Network. Retrieved December 3, 2007, from www. clickz.com/3584441

Related Workplace Issues. A major study done by Javelin Strategy and Research put the total losses from identification fraud at $49.3 billion in 2007. A Federal Trade Commission study showed that close to 8.3 million people were victims of identity theft in 2005.

Source

Privacy Rights Clearinghouse. *How many identity theft victims are there? What is the impact on victims?* Retrieved August 28, 2008, from www.privacyrights.org/ar/idtheftsurveys.htm

Digital Communication Facts

DEFINITION: *The electronic exchange of information*

Societal Incidents. Children using cell phones before, during, and after class have been reported as a major teacher concern. However, parents wanting the ability to communicate with their children and their safety concerns have caused school districts to rethink when and where cell phones can and should be used. A 2003 study by the Yankee Group, a research firm, found that 56% of 11- to 17-year-olds owned or shared a phone.

Source

Jeffrey Selingo. (2004, March 18). Hey kid, your backpack is ringing. *The New York Times*. Retrieved March 18, 2004, from www.nytimes.com/2004/03/18/technology/circuits/18kids.html

Related Workplace Issues. A study by Makovsky & Company in 2006 indicated that "the role of the blogosphere isn't yet fully realized by senior executives at Fortune 1000 companies. Reserved views extend both to blogging and how to respond to blog posts about the company."

"Of 150 top-level decision makers surveyed, 5% said they see corporate blogging as a communications medium; 3% see it as a brand-building technique; and less than 1% see it as a sales or lead-generation tool. Many respondents doubt the credibility of blogs as a communications tool (62%), a brand-building method (74%), or a sales or lead-generation channel (70%)."

Source

Enid Burns. (2006, May 9). *Executives slow to see value of corporate blogging*. The ClickZ Network. Retrieved December 3, 2007, from www.clickz.com/3604931

Digital Literacy Facts

DEFINITION: *The capability to use digital technology and knowing when and how to use it*

Societal Incidents. "Despite the assumption that today's college students are tech savvy and ICT literate, preliminary research released by ETS ... shows that many students lack the critical thinking skills to perform the kinds of information management and research tasks necessary for academic success," says Karen Bogan of ETS (Educational Testing Service).

Bogan continues: "Some of the most surprising preliminary research findings are that only 52% of test takers could correctly judge the objectivity of a website, and only 65% could correctly judge the site's authoritativeness. In a web search task, only 40% entered multiple search terms to narrow the results. And when selecting a research statement for a class assignment, only 44% identified a statement that captured the demands of the assignment."

Source

Karen Bogan. (2006). *College students fall short in demonstrating the ICT literacy skills necessary for success in college and the workplace.* ETS. Retrieved May 20, 2008, from http://findarticles. com/p/articles/mi_pwwi/is_200611/ai_n16840516

Related Workplace Issues. According to Meris Stansbury of *eSchool News*, "Americans are deeply concerned that the United States is not preparing students with the skills they need to compete in the new global economy…. Eighty-eight percent of voters say they believe schools can, and should, incorporate 21st-century skills such as critical thinking and problem solving, communication and self-direction, and computer and technology skills into the curriculum. What's more, 66% of voters say they believe students need more than just the basics of reading, writing, and math; schools also need to incorporate a broader range of skills, Americans say."

Source

Meris Stansbury. (2007, October 15). Voters urge teaching of 21st-century skills. *eSchool News.* Retrieved May 20, 2008, from www.eschoolnews.com/news/top-news/news-by-subject/research/?i=50114

Digital Etiquette Facts

DEFINITION: *The standards of conduct expected by other digital technology users*

Societal Incidents. A survey released by LetsTalk.com, a mobile retail and research company, found in 2006 that "only 2% say that using a cell phone in a movie or theater is acceptable, compared with 11% in 2000. Cell phone use in restaurants and public transportation is also slipping in approval, down to 21% and 45%, respectively. Cell phone use in supermarkets, however, is growing more acceptable, with 2 of every 3 people deeming it OK."

Source

Ryan Kim. (2006, February 27). The world's a cell-phone stage. *San Francisco Chronicle*. Retrieved December 5, 2007, from www.sfgate. com/cgi-bin/article.cgi?file=/c/a/2006/02/27/BUG2IHECTO1.DTL

Related Workplace Issues. From the office to the boardroom, you'll find many instances where digital etiquette comes into play. Early lapses were tolerated because of the perceived advantages to having the new gadgets, but now digital etiquette has become an issue in business for those using the technology as well as for those around them.

According to Marilyn Gardner of *The Christian Science Monitor*, "From the perspective of executives polled by Robert Half Technology, challenges exist. Two-thirds say that breaches in tech-etiquette are increasing. Nearly 90% think it is inappropriate to leave a cell phone ringer on during a business meeting, while 80% say sending instant messages or e-mail in meetings is a definite 'don't.' Two-thirds consider it poor etiquette to use personal computers during these sessions."

"Perhaps the biggest etiquette offenders, handheld devices allow users to check e-mail, search the web, send text messages, and make phone calls. These gadgets 'are causing normally polite people to commit egregious breaches of decorum,' says Peter Handal, chairman of Dale Carnegie Training. 'At meetings, people tend to get really annoyed by the use of BlackBerrys. I often see other people rolling their eyes'."

Source

Marilyn Gardner. (2006, April 17). Etiquette's electronic frontier. *The Christian Science Monitor.* Retrieved January 18, 2008, from www.csmonitor.com/2006/0417/p14s01-stct.html

Digital Law Facts

DEFINITION: *The legal rights and restrictions governing technology use*

Societal Incidents. Downloading programs and music illegally from the Internet has become a serious concern of educators. A survey by Harris Interactive (commissioned by the Business Software Alliance), reported that a large majority of children (88% from ages 8 to 18) know that most popular music is copyrighted, but 56% download it anyway.

Source

David McGuire. (2004, May 18). *Report:* Kids pirate music freely. *The Washington Post.* Retrieved May 20, 2008, from www.washingtonpost.com/wp-dyn/articles/A37231–2004May18. html

Related Workplace Issues. Groups such as the RIAA (Recording Industry Association of American) and the MPAA (Motion Picture Association of America) have attempted to crack down on those who steal music and video files. The Business Software Alliance reported that software piracy alone cost the United States $1.9 billion in 2002. Another study by Ipsos showed that 66% of college faculty and administrators say it is wrong to download or swap files; yet fewer than 25% of students at the same colleges say it is wrong.

Source

InternetNews.com. (2003). *Study: Colleges a gateway to software piracy.* Retrieved May 20, 2008, from www.Internetnews.com/stats/ article.php/3078651

Digital Rights and Responsibilities Facts

DEFINITION: *The privileges and freedoms extended to all digital technology users, and the behavioral expectations that come with them*

Societal Incidents. In the 2003–2004 school year, i-SAFE America, a nonprofit foundation that focuses on Internet safety education, surveyed students from across the country on the topic of cyberbullying. According to the report, "It is a topic that not many adults were talking about. It turns out to be a topic all too familiar with students."

"Bullying is no longer about the strong picking on the weak in the schoolyard. The physical assault has been replaced by a 24 hour per day, 7 days a week online bashing. Savvy students are using instant messaging, e-mails, chat rooms, and websites they create to humiliate a peer. No longer can parents count on seeing the tell-tale physical signs of bullying—a black eye, bloody lip, torn clothes. But the damage done by cyberbullies is no less real, and can be infinitely more painful."

Cyberbullying Statistics
(based on a 2004 i-SAFE survey of 1,500 students Grades 4–8)

- 42% of kids have been bullied while online. 1 in 4 have had it happen more than once.

- 35% of kids have been threatened online. Nearly 1 in 5 have had it happen more than once.

- 21% of kids have received mean or threatening e-mail or other messages.

- 58% of kids admit someone has said mean or hurtful things to them online. More than 4 out of 10 say it has happened more than once.

- 53% of kids admit having said something mean or hurtful to another person online. More than 1 in 3 have done it more than once.

- 58% have not told their parents or an adult about something mean or hurtful that happened to them online.

Source

i-SAFE. (No date). *Cyber bullying: Statistics and tips.* Retrieved May 20, 2008, from www.isafe.org/channels/sub. php?ch=op&sub_id=media_cyber_bullying

Related Workplace Issues. A study done by Hitwise in 2003 found that of those who view sexually explicit material on the Internet, 72% surveyed access the sites at home while 28% view this content in the workplace. Another study by N2H2 showed growth of pornographic pages from 14 million in 1998 to roughly 260 million in 2003.

Source

Robyn Greenspan. (2003). *Porn pages reach 260 million.* InternetNews.com. Retrieved May 20, 2008, from www. Internetnews.com/bus-news/article.php/3083001

Digital Health and Wellness Facts

DEFINITION: *The elements of physical and psychological well-being related to digital technology use*

Societal Incidents. Children today are going to be the workforce of tomorrow. A 2002 study done by Peter Buckle, of the Robens Centre for Health Ergonomics at the University of Surrey in England, reported that children are "already damaged." He found that 36% of 11- to 14-year-olds suffer serious, ongoing back pain. Buckle added, "Children are at even greater risk because they are spending more and more time in front of a computer."

Source

> CBC News. (2002, September 12). *Children suffer back pain because of computers.* Canadian Broadcasting Corporation. Retrieved December 3, 2004, from www.cbc.ca/news/story/2002/09/11/Computerskids_020911.html

Related Workplace Issues. In 2002, Dr. Fredrick Gerr at Emory University in Atlanta reported in an article in the *American Journal of Industrial Medicine* that more than half of computer users developed neck or shoulder symptoms during the first year on a new job. The results showed nearly 40% of participants developed hand or arm symptoms while using a computer and 21% actually developed a disorder.

Source

> CBC News. (2002, April 4). *Pain from computer use more common than thought: Study.* Canadian Broadcasting Corporation. Retrieved May 20, 2008, from www.cbc.ca/health/story/2002/04/29/computer_pain020429.html

Digital Security Facts

DEFINITION: *The precautions that all technology users must take to guarantee their personal safety and the security of their network*

Societal Incidents. Although concerns over personal data security have not diminished, the 2006 ChoiceStream Personalization Survey found that more than half of the respondents are inclined to provide demographic and other personal information in exchange for a personalized online experience, reports Enid Burns of the ClickZ Network.

Burns continues: "Personalization and privacy go hand in hand. In the past year, consumer interest in a more personalized experience has increased by 24% to 57% of respondents to the recent survey. Consumers willing to let a site track clicks, purchases, and other behavior increased by 34% in the same period. Concerns over personal data security, however, remained largely unchanged. Sixty-two percent of respondents express concern, compared to 63% in the 2005 survey."

Source

Enid Burns. (2007, January 10). *Personalization desire outweighs security concerns.* The ClickZ Network. Retrieved December 5, 2007, from www.clickz.com/3624484

Related Workplace Issues. According to Enid Burns of the ClickZ Network, "The greatest asset under threat by spyware infections is believed to be the integrity of intellectual property and customers' personally identifiable information. Yet companies have incentive to protect against spyware threats. A series of studies conducted by the CMO Council show how security issues threaten brand loyalty and how brands can excel by having crisis containment measures in place."

"Threats lie in spyware detection, removal, and prevention. Eighty-three percent of respondents said their employers have active day-to-day spyware prevention programs in place. Of those companies with prevention plans happening daily, 24% say the measures taken are technology-based spyware detection or prevention solutions."

Source

Enid Burns. (2006, November 14). *Intellectual property threatened by spyware*. The ClickZ Network. Retrieved December 5, 2007, from www.clickz.com/3623943

CHAPTER 7

Web 2.0?
What Happened to Web 1.0?

Web 2.0 is one of the latest buzzwords to hit the Net, but even in the field of technology the concept of Web 2.0 is often misunderstood. Wikipedia states:

> *Web 2.0* is a term describing the trend in the use of World Wide Web technology and web design that aims to enhance creativity, information sharing, and, most notably, collaboration among users. These concepts have led to the development and evolution of web-based communities and hosted services, such as social networking sites, wikis, blogs, and folksonomies…. Although the term suggests a new version of the World Wide Web, it does not refer to an update to any technical specifications, but to changes in the ways software developers and end-users use the web.

So what are some of these changes in the way people use the web? Wikipedia further explains:

> Technologies such as weblogs, social bookmarking, wikis, podcasts, RSS feeds (and other forms of many-to-many publishing), social software, web

application programming interfaces (APIs), and online web services such as eBay and Gmail provide a significant enhancement over read-only websites.

Now you might be wondering: Does Web 2.0 affect our children?

The answer is yes. It does affect our children because many are already using these tools. And there is good reason to be interested in Web 2.0 sites verses the old "read-only" sites. Web 2.0 offers the ability to interact, not just with others, but with the sites themselves. The big draws for Web 2.0 are the communication and the interaction. These are also the reasons parents need to be aware of these tools.

The social aspect of Web 2.0 leads many to participate as they might among a close group of friends, which can open them to certain dangers. Social networking sites such as MySpace, Friendster, and Facebook allow kids to share information with their peers, which may be acceptable, depending on the kind of information that is shared. When pictures are posted or comments are made online, they can be seen by anyone with an Internet connection (unless privacy safeguards are in place). Providing too much personal information can lead to online harassment or cyberstalking.

Kids may post their address, phone number, birth date, and other personal information at social networking sites. With this basic information, identities can be stolen. Often kids have no idea what has happened until they want to apply for credit, and by then it is too late.

Some postings may be outside a child's control, such as others posting pictures or information on their own social site without the child's knowledge. This can amount to teasing or gossip, or worse, harassment and cyberbullying.

Many organizations—such as businesses, colleges, and law enforcement agencies—spend time at these sites to determine whether people have posted illegal or immoral information. People can lose out on jobs or opportunities (such as athletic scholarships) because of what is posted.

Clearly, children need rules about the information they post on social networking sites. Parents need to talk to their children about what they're posting and even go to their sites to see what is posted. Some parents may think that this is an invasion of their child's privacy, but it is not. If you can see the information as a parent, anyone with an Internet connection and access to the site can also see it. Kids may not understand why anyone would want to see their personal information or pay attention to what they say to their friends. Online stalking and identity theft are just a couple of reasons.

Another Web 2.0 topic that should be of interest to parents is P2P (peer-to-peer). WhatIs.com explains:

> On the Internet, peer-to-peer (referred to as P2P) is a type of transient Internet network that allows a group of computer users with the same networking program to connect with each other and directly access files from one another's hard drives. Napster and Gnutella are examples of this kind of peer-to-peer software. Major producers of content, including record companies, have shown their concern about what they consider illegal sharing of copyrighted content by suing some P2P users.

P2P offers many opportunities for communication and efficiency, but as the definition here indicates, there is a downside as well. P2P allows the sharing of copyrighted files, such as music and movies, which is a violation of copyright laws. The RIAA (Recording Industry Association of America) and the MPAA (Motion Picture Association of America) are tracking down movie and music pirates and leveling large fines (up to $10,000 per instance). One case has even gone as far as the Supreme Court, which has found in favor of the recording industry.

The idea behind P2P is to create a "network," or connection, between computers. When you become part of this network, all the information on your computer can potentially be shared by everyone, including social security numbers (if you do your taxes on a home computer) and banking information (if you do your banking online). Another concern with some P2P sites is that viruses or spyware (software code that shares information from your computer) could be downloaded to your computer—yet another reason to stay up-to-date with your virus and spyware protection.

It may appear that I'm suggesting that Web 2.0 applications are inappropriate for use by anyone. This is not true. Web 2.0 offers many benefits: collaboration with wikis, self-expression through blogging, and receiving regular updates with RSS (Really Simple Syndication), to name just a few. Many of these tools are useful not just at home but in the classroom as well (such as sharing ideas on blogs or developing writing skills using wikis). Like any technology, they have positive and negative aspects. It's up to parents to be involved in their children's use of technology and to make decisions that are in their best interests.

Technology will continue to change and become more complex. Before too long I'm sure we'll see a Web 3.0. It is important for us as parents to keep current with the changes that affect our children.

Sources

Wikipedia. (No date). *Web 2.0*. Retrieved June 3, 2008, from http://en.wikipedia.org/wiki/Web_2.0

WhatIs.com. (No date). *Peer-to-peer*. Retrieved July 22, 2008, from http://searchnetworking.techtarget.com/sDefinition/0,,sid7_gci212769,00.html

Blogs

The word *blog* originated from a shortening of the phrase "web log." The most simplistic view of a blog is that it is an online diary. A large number of blogs are just that, an individual's account of his or her day, pets, relationships, or opinions about current events. But blogs can be much more than this. Because many allow readers to post comments and all allow entries to be linked to by other bloggers, the "blogosphere" is a communal space that promotes and sustains dialogue among any number of users with common interests.

This creates many opportunities for education and collaboration. If guided and encouraged correctly, students can use blogs to write stories, gather information, share data, and negotiate differing opinions and disagreements. Teachers and administrators can use blogs to share information with parents, make announcements, or create a forum for discussion.

In the home, a blog can allow your child to be self-expressive and share information with friends. The main thing to remember is that many of the "no cost" blogs are open and available to anyone with web access. Because of this, parents need to read what their children are writing on their blogs. (Some children will see this as a violation of their privacy, but if parents can see the content, so can anyone in the world. Demonstrating the openness of blogs can serve as a lesson on the importance of children understanding the technology they use.)

The following list provides several links related to blogs. The best way to learn about blogs, however, is to visit one or several and see what people are writing about. Keep in mind that a wide range of blogs are available and that many different kinds of people post to them. Some people will blog about very mundane topics, while others may discuss very open and experimental ideas. Be prepared to see a wide range of topics.

Education Blogs

Blogs in Education
    http://awd.cl.uh.edu/blog/

Landmark's Class Blogmeister
    www.classblogmeister.com
    Blogmeister allows educators to take a look at student blogs before they post.

Weblogg-ed
    www.Weblogg-ed.com

Blog Directories

(Note: Some material on these websites may not be suitable for all users.)

Blogwise Directory
    www.blogwise.com

eTalkinghead Political Blog Directory
    www.directory.etalkinghead.com

Articles about Blogs in Education

Blogging 101
    www.unc.edu/~zuiker/blogging101/

Using Blogs in the Classroom
    http://husd4-tr.blogspot.com

Really Simple Syndication (RSS)

Once you have an understanding of blogs, you are ready to move on to Really Simple Syndication, or RSS. An RSS feed allows people to receive automatic updates on new postings to a blog, news site, or any other RSS-enabled site. Look for an icon like any of these:

Podcasts can also be syndicated using RSS, so regular listeners can be notified when a new podcast is available.

Major newspapers (such as *The New York Times*) and other traditional media outlets have created RSS feeds to their content. Once you have set up your account with an RSS aggregator or "feed reader," any feeds that you subscribe to will send updates directly to your account.

Creating an RSS feed does not have to be an overly complex process. The following site provides the basics on how to use a popular web-based program to syndicate your blog or podcast: www.speedofcreativity. org/2006/02/28/podcast37-effective-school-podcasting/.

The nice thing about RSS is that people are able to customize exactly what they want to receive. If they want news from one source, sports from another, and technology information from another, it's easy to do that using a feed reader. You can also receive feeds from several sources on the same topic to create your own customized newspaper.

The benefits for education are plentiful. Teachers can subscribe to feeds on topics they are currently covering in class and receive the latest information as it happens.

Schools can also create their own RSS feed for teachers, parents, and students, eliminating the need to send out hundreds of e-mails.

RSS Resources

RSS Readers
> http://blogspace.com/rss/readers/

RSS WebReference
> www.Webreference.com/authoring/languages/xml/rss/

What is RSS?
> http://rss.softwaregarden.com/aboutrss.html

Podcasting

To understand podcasting, you first need to understand blogging (see the Blogs section). In simple terms, podcasting is audio blogging. Instead of writing out information, podcasters record and post audio files on the Internet, where they are available for anyone who wants to listen to them.

Podcasting has its roots in the Apple community. The original podcasts were for Apple iPods, but today, any device that can play MP3 files can also play podcasts. The process for creating a podcast can be as complex or as simple as the user wants it to be. Several good audio-editing programs are available that can help you make more professional-sounding recordings and eliminate the "ums" and mistakes. Once the audio file is recorded, it needs to be saved or converted to the MP3 format. To learn more about creating a basic podcast and to find resources for doing so, see www.speedofcreativity.org/2006/02/28/podcast37-effective-school-podcasting/.

As always, the best way to learn a new skill is to use it. If you do not have an iPod or other MP3 player, don't despair: most computers can play MP3 files. The Landmarks for Schools site (http://landmark-project.com/) has several educational podcasts that you might find interesting, or try David Warlick's site (http://davidwarlick.com/podcasts/). This site allows you to play the podcast right in the browser window, with no download required.

What are the implications for parents, students, and schools? Take a look at the Edupodder Weblog: http://weblog.edupodder.com/2004/11/podcasting-in-education.html. The author, Steve Sloan, explores the many ways that podcasting can support educational objectives: distance learning, additional support for special needs students, and make-up classes, among others. Some universities are providing podcasts from courses at no charge.

Hundreds of podcasts are available, on just about any topic of interest. Podcasts teach everything from foreign languages to playing the guitar. This medium allows information to be carried with kids on their MP3 players, wherever they might be.

Wikis

According to one wiki information site, "Wiki is Hawaiian for 'quick.' Wiki is also a software tool that allows users to freely create and edit hyperlinked web pages using a web browser. Wiki [software] typically uses a simple syntax for users to create new pages and crosslinks between pages on the fly. In addition to the main open source version there are also many noncommercial and commercial clones and some 'wiki farms' (places where you can set up a wiki without needing your own server)."

The wiki is a powerful tool for collaboration. One user can begin the development of a document or information page, and then other users can add to or make modifications to that document. A record of all changes and additions is kept (along with who made them). The most famous example of a wiki is the online encyclopedia Wikipedia (http://wikipedia.org).

Wikis can be used in classrooms for creating collaborative writing projects. For example, students can create their own study guides for the class. One student places some information on the wiki and others can update that information or add their own. Students can create a glossary of key terms, a timeline of critical events, a catalogue of important characters, or a list of essential formulas. Because the wiki resides on the Internet, it is always available to students and their parents.

Just like any digital information, children need to be discerning of what wiki information they take as the truth. Because wikis can be so easily created and changed, false information can easily be posted. As with other web pages, parents and kids need to come up with a way to identify what information is true and what is not.

Wikis require a bit more time and computer savvy than blogs or podcasts, but they can offer amazing returns in student learning and motivation when used well.

Wiki Resources

seedwiki
> http://seedwiki.com

The Teachers' Lounge
> http://teacherslounge.editme.com

Wikis, in Collaborative Learning Environments Sourcebook
> www.criticalmethods.org/collab/v.mv?d=1_34

Source

M. Terre Blanche. (2004). *Wikis.* Collaborative learning environment sourcebook. Retrieved September 29, 2004, from www.criticalmethods.org/collab/v.mv?d=1_34

CHAPTER 8

Conclusion

This book provides a starting point for parents to think about how children should use technology. You now have a strong foundation, yet even with all this information some topics may require further exploration on your part. That is to be expected. With the complex and changing nature of technology, it would be impossible to cover every scenario of appropriate and inappropriate use. However, with the digital citizenship framework provided in this book, parents can talk to their children about the fundamental issues surrounding technology use.

Digital citizenship is important in all areas of society—at home, at school, at work, and at play (see Target for teaching digital citizenship figure). The evidence of poor behavior with technology documented in newspapers, in magazines, on TV, and online provides proof that these issues must be addressed or more problems will occur. It is important for parents to be at the forefront of digital citizenship, because parents are preparing the next generation of technology users. By understanding how we all are affected by inappropriate technology use, we can prepare kids today to work with others around the world.

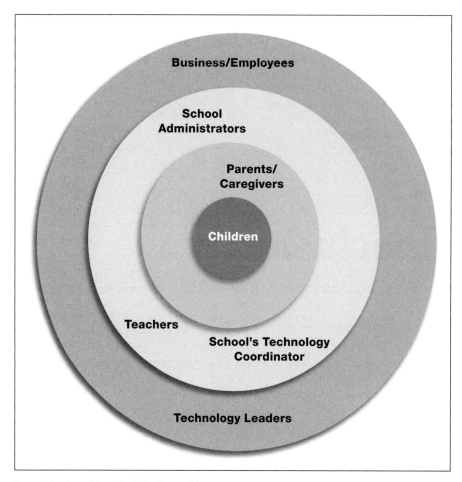

Target for teaching digital citizenship

Digital Citizenship and Education

Parents and educators must keep open lines of communication about digital citizenship in order to provide a consistent message to children. Granted, there may be different rules for technology use at home and at school, but the basic concepts of appropriate use should be the same. If teachers and parents are able to talk about technology utilizing the same vocabulary, it will be easier to understand how they each are asking kids to use the technology.

For example, if parents know that schools are limiting the use of social networking sites (and understand why), then they too can be aware when their children are using these sites at home and know what to look for to counter potential problems. Many districts have limited what students can do in school through the use of firewalls and network restrictions, but kids may have full access when they get home. Parents need to know where the policies of the school end and theirs begin.

Find out how the digital citizenship message is being shared with your children at school. If no plan is in place, ask that a program be provided so that all children can be prepared to enter a digital society.

Digital Citizenship and Business

Many instances of inappropriate technology use occur throughout business and industry. Statistics show that billions of dollars are lost each year through the inappropriate use of technology. These loses are in real dollars and in productivity. The costs can be attributed to issues of digital security (information is lost because of viruses), digital rights and responsibilities (productivity is down because people watch pornography at work), digital communication (work time is squandered through texting or chatting), and digital health and welfare (employees become injured from repetitive stress activities). The list goes on and on.

Quite simply, when people use technology inappropriately at work, the company loses money. A strong digital citizenship program at home and at school could rectify some of these problems.

Digital Citizenship and the Law

Digital technology has had an enormous effect on every level of our society. There is no doubt that with the help of digital technology we have made great strides in productivity, creativity, and efficiency; but there are always those who choose to use technology for less appropriate reasons. Inappropriate uses have flourished in the absence of a set of norms for this rapidly shifting landscape. As a consequence, laws to regulate digital technologies are arriving on the scene. Most often these laws are written to protect users and their property, but as the years tick by and technology continues to advance, everything from copyright infringement to where and when you can talk on a cell phone are increasingly falling under legal jurisdiction.

Respecting and following the laws related to technology use is one aspect of digital citizenship, but there's more to it than that. Digital citizenship includes understanding the reasons for having such rules. Technology users should think about what is acceptable and, after reflecting on the situation, do the right thing. But some digital technology users (especially children) may not be able to understand why they should not do something when they have the ability to do it. The goal of this book is to help create citizens who learn these justifications early in their life, so that later on, as they grow older, they will not have to guess about whether something is appropriate. They will have the tools to evaluate digital technology situations and come to the correct conclusions.

All digital technology users need to have a strong foundation in digital citizenship. We should expect, and work to create, citizens who realize that technology affects not only themselves, but those around them. We will always need laws and policies on technology use, but it will be our own understanding of digital technology and how we use it that will define our future.

Coming of Age in a Digital World

As a parent, I have observed the amazing gateways that technology opens up for my children. When I was growing up, getting my driver's license was my opportunity for freedom. But my children did not see getting a driver's license as the same "coming of age" ritual. When my children became teenagers, the discussion was not about when they could get their driver's license, but about when they could get a chat account, an Xbox game, or a cell phone. My license represented the opportunity to drive where I wanted. My children have the world at their fingertips, so why would they need to go anywhere? This new generation seems to be more concerned with connecting to each other in a "virtual world" than getting out into the "real world."

Technology is opening many doors, but it is also ushering in new ways of looking at communication, etiquette, law, and other social forces. The challenge for parents (and children as well) is to determine how to navigate successfully within the changing environment.

As technology becomes more "invisible" or commonplace, it will be even harder for children to realize the need for being a good digital citizen. As more and newer technology comes out, we cannot allow our children to become so comfortable with its use that they forget their responsibilities as digital citizens. They will say they "already know what to do" or "that's old stuff," but if they have not learned good digital citizenship, appropriate technology use will continue to be an issue.

Parents need a roadmap for the technology future. The next few years will bring many changes to how we all look at technology. Now is the time to start the discussion. Now is the time to look to the future. Technology is not going away, and it will be parents who decide how technology will be viewed by their children. We can't turn our backs and believe that technology does not exist. We must embrace technology and prepare our children to become citizens of a digital society—digital citizens.

References

Berniker, M. (2003). *Study: ID theft often goes unrecognized.* InternetNews.com. Retrieved May 20, 2008, from www.Internetnews.com/stats/article.php/3081881

Bogan, K. (2006). *College students fall short in demonstrating the ICT literacy skills necessary for success in college and the workplace.* ETS. Retrieved May 20, 2008, from http://findarticles.com/p/articles/mi_pwwi/is_200611/ai_n16840516

Bridis, T. (2004, November 23). *Growth of high-speed Internet disappoints some experts.* USA Today, p. 7A. Retrieved May 20, 2008, from www.usatoday. com/tech/news/2004–11–22-high-speed-connections_x.htm

Burns, E. (2006, February 10). *Online ads influence collegiate set.* The ClickZ Network. Retrieved December 3, 2007, from www.clickz.com/3584441

Burns, E. (2006, May 9). *Executives slow to see value of corporate blogging.* The ClickZ Network. Retrieved December 3, 2007, from www.clickz.com/3604931

Burns, E. (2006, November 14). *Intellectual property threatened by spyware.* The ClickZ Network. Retrieved December 5, 2007, from www.clickz.com/3623943

Burns, E. (2007, January 10). *Personalization desire outweighs security concerns.* The ClickZ Network. Retrieved December 5, 2007, from www.clickz.com/3624484

Burns, E. (2007, December 14). *Online holiday sales peak in afternoon, sales up 19 percent.* The ClickZ Network. Retrieved January 18, 2008, from www.clickz.com/showPage.html?page=3627887

CBC News. (2002, September 12). *Children suffer back pain because of computers.* Canadian Broadcasting Corporation. Retrieved December 3, 2004, from www.cbc.ca/news/story/2002/09/11/Computerskids_020911.html

CBC News. (2002, April 4). *Pain from computer use more common than thought: Study.* Canadian Broadcasting Corporation. Retrieved May 20, 2008, from www.cbc.ca/health/story/2002/04/29/computer_pain020429.html

ConsumerConfidence.org.uk. (No date). *Safe online purchases.* Retrieved May 26, 2008, from www.consumerconfidence.org.uk/safe-online-purchasing.html

Fox, S., & Livingston, G. (2007, March 14). *Latinos online.* Pew Internet & American Life Project. Retrieved May 20, 2008, from http://pewresearch.org/pubs/429/latinos-online

Friedman, T. (2005). *The world is flat.* New York. Farrar, Straus, and Giroux.

Gardner, M. (2006, April 17). *Etiquette's electronic frontier.* The Christian Science Monitor. Retrieved January 18, 2008, from www.csmonitor.com/2006/0417/p14s01-stct.html

Greenspan, R. (2003). *Porn pages reach 260 million.* InternetNews.com. Retrieved May 20, 2008, from www.Internetnews.com/bus-news/article.php/3083001

International Society for Technology in Education (ISTE). (No date). *National educational technology standards.* Retrieved June 17, 2008, from www.iste.org/AM/Template.cfm?Section=NETS

InternetNews.com. (2003). *Study: Colleges a gateway to software piracy.* Retrieved May 20, 2008, from www.Internetnews.com/stats/article.php/3078651

i-SAFE. (No date). *Cyber bullying: Statistics and tips.* Retrieved May 20, 2008, from www.isafe.org/channels/sub.php?ch=op&sub_id=media_cyber_bullying

Kim, R. (2006, February 27). *The world's a cell-phone stage.* San Francisco Chronicle. Retrieved December 5, 2007, from www.sfgate.com/cgi-bin/article cgi?file=/c/a/2006/02/27/BUG2IHECTO1.DTL

Landsberger, J. (No date). *Webtruth: Evaluating Website content.* Study Guides and Strategies. Retrieved August 15, 2008, from www.studygs.net/evaluate.htm

McGuire, D. (2004, May 18). *Report: Kids pirate music freely.* The Washington Post. Retrieved May 20, 2008, from www.washingtonpost.com/wp-dyn/articles/A37231–2004May18.html

Media Awareness Network. (2008). *Instant messaging.* Retrieved July 28, 2008, from www.media-awareness.ca/english/parents/Internet/safe_passage_parents/messaging_safety_p.cfm

Norton. (2007, March 12). *Your kids, the Internet, and the law.* Retrieved August 15, 2008, from www.symantec.com/norton/products/library/article.jsp?aid=kids_Internet_and_law

Norwood School. (No date). *Top tips for computer protection at home.* Retrieved May 27, 2008, from http://library.norwoodschool.org/Help_FAQs/home_computing/top_tips_protection.htm

Peters, T. (2008). *Bridging the digital divide.* Bridges.org. Retrieved January 12, 2008, from http://usinfo.state.gov/journals/itgic/1103/ijge/gj08.htm

Prensky, M. (2001). Digital natives, digital immigrants. *On the Horizon, 9*(5), 10–15.

Privacy Rights Clearinghouse. *How many identity theft victims are there? What is the impact on victims?* Retrieved August 28, 2008, from www.privacyrights.org/ar/idtheftsurveys.htm

SafeComputingTips.com. (No date). *Child ergonomics.* Retrieved May 27, 2008, from http://safecomputingtips.com/child-ergonomics.html

SafeKids.com. (No date). *Family Contract for Online Safety.* (Kid's pledge adapted from the brochure Child Safety on the Information Highway, by Lawrence J. Magid.) Retrieved August 16, 2008, from http://safekids. com/family-contract-for-online-safety/

Selingo, J. (2004, March 18). *Hey kid, your backpack is ringing.* The New York Times. Retrieved March 18, 2004, from www.nytimes.com/2004/03/18/technology/ circuits/18kids.html

Stansbury, M. (2007, October 15). *Voters urge teaching of 21st-century skills.* eSchool News. Retrieved May 20, 2008, from www.eschoolnews. com/news/top-news/news-by-subject/research/?i=50114

TeacherVision. (No date). *Netiquette.* Retrieved August 15, 2008, from www. teachervision.fen.com/tv/printables/netguide31_33.pdf

Terre Blanche, M. (2004). *Wikis.* Collaborative learning environment sourcebook. Retrieved September 29, 2004, from www.criticalmethods.org/collab/v.mv?d=1_34

WhatIs.com. (No date). *Peer-to-peer.* Retrieved July 22, 2008, from http:// searchnetworking.techtarget.com/sDefinition/0,,sid7_gci212769,00.html

Wikipedia. (No date). *Web 2.0.* Retrieved June 3, 2008, from http://en.wikipedia. org/wiki/Web_2.0

Definition of Terms

acceptable use policy (AUP). "Policy set up by the network administrator or other school leaders in conjunction with their technology needs and safety concerns. This policy restricts the manner in which a network may be used and provides guidelines for teachers using technology in the classroom." (4Teachers.org)

adware. "A form of spyware that collects information about the user in order to display advertisements in the web browser based on the information it collects from the user's browsing patterns." (Webopedia)

blog (from web log). "A website that contains dated text entries in reverse chronological order (most recent first) about a particular topic. Blogs serve many purposes from online newsletters to personal journals to 'ranting and raving.' They can be written by one person or a group of contributors. Entries contain commentary and links to other websites, and images as well as a search facility may be included. Blogs may also contain video (vlog)." (TechWeb)

browser. See web browser.

cellular telephone (or cell phone) service. "Type of short-wave analog or digital telecommunication in which a subscriber has a wireless connection from a mobile telephone to a relatively nearby transmitter. The transmitter's span of coverage is called a cell." (WhatIs.com)

chat room. "An interactive, online discussion (by keyboard) about a specific topic that is hosted on the Internet or on a BBS. On the Internet, chat rooms are available from major services such as AOL, individual websites, and the Internet Relay Chat (IRC) system—the Internet's traditional computer conferencing system. Chat rooms are set up to handle group discussions, and everyone sees what everyone else types in, although two people can decide to break off and have their own keyboard chat. Instant messaging, a similar concept, works in an opposite manner. With instant messaging, two people normally interact back and forth and must specifically invite others to join in." (TechWeb)

citizen. "Person who works against injustice, not for individual recognition or personal advantage, but for the benefit of all people. In realizing this task— shattering privileges, ensuring information and competence, acting in favor of all—each person becomes a citizen." (Johnson & Nissenbaum)

computer ethics. "Analysis of the nature and social impact of computer technology and the corresponding formulation and justification of policies for the ethical use of such technology." (Johnson & Nissenbaum)

computer literacy. "Level of expertise and familiarity someone has with computers. Computer literacy generally refers to the ability to use applications rather than to program. Individuals who are very computer literate are sometimes called power users." (Webopedia)

cyberspace. "Metaphor for describing the nonphysical terrain created by computer systems. Online systems, for example, create a cyberspace within which people can communicate with one another (by e-mail), do research, or simply window shop. Like physical space, cyberspace contains objects (files, mail messages, graphics, etc.) and different modes of transportation and delivery. Unlike real space, though, exploring cyberspace does not require any physical movement other than pressing keys on a keyboard or moving a mouse. The term was coined by author William Gibson in his sci-fi novel *Neuromancer* (1984)." (Webopedia)

digital. "System based on discontinuous data or events. Computers are digital machines because at their most basic level they can distinguish between just two values, 0 and 1, or off and on. There is no simple way to represent all the values in between, such as 0.25. All data that a computer processes must be encoded digitally, as a series of zeroes and ones. Internally, computers are digital because they consist of discrete units called bits that are either on or off. But by combining many bits in complex ways, computers simulate analog events. In one sense, this is what computer science is all about." (Webopedia)

digital divide. "Discrepancy between people who have access to and the resources to use new information and communication tools, such as the Internet, and people who do not have the resources and access to the technology. The term also describes the discrepancy between those who have the skills, knowledge, and abilities to use the technologies and those who do not. The digital divide can exist between those living in rural areas and those living in urban areas, between the educated and uneducated, between economic classes, and on a global scale between more and less industrially developed nations." (Webopedia)

distance learning. "Type of education, typically college-level, in which students work on their own at home or at the office and communicate with faculty and other students through e-mail, electronic forums, videoconferencing, chat rooms, bulletin boards, instant messaging, and other forms of computer-based communication. Most distance learning programs include a computer-based training (CBT) system and communications tools to produce a virtual classroom. Because the Internet and World Wide Web are accessible from virtually all computer platforms, they serve as the foundation for many distance learning systems." (Webopedia)

download. "To save a file onto your computer from another source, like the Internet. People often download files, such as freeware, shareware, installation software, sounds, movie clips, text files, or news streams, onto their computer for viewing or listening." (4Teachers.org)

e-commerce (electronic commerce). "Buying and selling goods and services on the Internet, especially the World Wide Web." (WhatIs.com)

e-mail (electronic mail). "Transmission of messages over communications networks. The messages can be notes entered from the keyboard or electronic files stored on disk. Most mainframes, minicomputers, and computer networks have an e-mail system. Some electronic-mail systems are confined to a single computer system or network, but others have gateways to other computer systems, enabling users to send electronic mail anywhere in the world. Companies that are fully computerized make extensive use of e-mail because it is fast, flexible, and reliable." (Webopedia)

ergonomics. "The science of fitting the workplace to the worker. Ergonomics involves reducing exposure to physical trauma, redesigning tools and workstations, and preventing and treating cumulative trauma disorders (CTDs), such as carpal tunnel syndrome and tendonitis." (Occupational and Environmental Health Center)

firewall. "Hardware and/or software that separates a local area network (LAN) into two or more parts for security purposes." (4Teachers.org)

handheld computer. "Portable computer that is small enough to be held in one's hand. Although extremely convenient to carry, handheld computers have not replaced notebook computers because of their small keyboards and screens. The most popular handheld computers are those that are specifically designed to provide PIM (personal information manager) functions, such as a calendar and address book. Some manufacturers are trying to solve the small keyboard problem by replacing the keyboard with an electronic pen. However, these pen-based devices rely on handwriting recognition technologies, which are still in their infancy." (Webopedia)

home page. "Page on the Internet that most often gives users access to the rest of the website. A site is a collection of pages." (4Teachers.org)

information highway. "Buzzword to describe the Internet, bulletin board services, online services, and other services that enable people to obtain information from telecommunications networks. In the U.S., there is currently a national debate about how to shape and control these avenues of information. Many people believe that the information highway should be designed and regulated by government, just like conventional highway systems. Others argue that government should adopt a more laissez-faire attitude. Nearly everyone agrees that accessing the information highway is going to be a normal part of everyday life in the near future." (Webopedia)

information literacy. "Ability to locate, evaluate, and use information to become independent lifelong learners." (Southern Association of Colleges and Schools)

instant messaging (IM). "Exchanging text messages in real time between two or more people logged into a particular instant messaging (IM) service. Instant messaging is more interactive than e-mail because messages are sent immediately, whereas e-mail messages can be queued up in a mail server for seconds or minutes. However, there are no elaborate page layout options in instant messaging as there are with e-mail. The IM text box is short, and pressing the enter key often sends the text. IM is designed for fast text interaction." (TechWeb)

Internet. "Global network connecting millions of computers. More than 100 countries are linked into exchanges of data, news, and opinions." (Webopedia)

iPod. "Apple's iPod is a small portable music player. Users can transfer songs to their iPod with their computer, iTunes, and the iPod software." (Webopedia)

IT (information technology). "Pronounced as separate letters, IT refers to the broad subject concerned with all aspects of managing and processing information, especially within a large organization or company. Because computers are central to information management, computer departments within companies and universities are often called IT departments. Some companies refer to this department as IS (information services) or MIS (management information services)." (Webopedia)

keystroke logging (keylogging). "A method of capturing and recording user keystrokes. Keylogging can be useful to determine sources of errors in computer systems, to study how users interact and access with systems, and is sometimes used to measure employee productivity on certain clerical tasks. Such systems are also highly useful for law enforcement and espionage—for instance, providing a means to obtain passwords or encryption keys and thus bypassing other security measures. Keyloggers are widely available on the Internet. There are currently two types of keylogging methods, hardware and software based." (Wikipedia)

"Although keylogger programs are promoted for benign purposes like allowing parents to monitor their children's whereabouts on the Internet, most privacy advocates agree that the potential for abuse is so great that legislation should be enacted to clearly make the unauthorized use of keyloggers a criminal offense." (WhatIs.com)

mobile phone. See cellular telephone.

MP3. "The name of the file extension and also the name of the type of file for MPEG, audio layer 3. Layer 3 is one of three coding schemes (layer 1, layer 2, and layer 3) for the compression of audio signals. Because MP3 files are small, they can easily be transferred across the Internet." (Webopedia)

Napster. "An online music file-sharing service created by Shawn Fanning while he was attending Northeastern University in Boston and operating between June 1999 and July 2001. It was the first widely used peer-to-peer sharing service, and it made a major impact on how people, especially university students, used the Internet. Its technology allowed music fans to easily share MP3 format song files with each other, thus leading to the music industry's accusations of massive copyright violations. Although the original service was shut down by court order, it paved the way for decentralized peer-to-peer file-sharing programs, which have been much harder to control. The service was named *Napster* after Fanning's nickname. Napster's brand and logo were purchased after the company closed its doors and continue to be used by a pay service." (Wikipedia)

netiquette. "Contraction of *Internet etiquette*, the etiquette guidelines for posting messages to online services, and particularly Internet newsgroups. Netiquette covers not only rules to maintain civility in discussions (i.e., avoiding flames), but also special guidelines unique to the electronic nature of forum messages. For example, netiquette advises users to use simple formats because complex formatting may not appear correctly for all readers. In most cases, netiquette is enforced by fellow users who will vociferously object if you break a rule of netiquette." (Webopedia)

phishing. "Pronounced 'fishing.' A scam designed to steal valuable information such as credit card and social security numbers, user IDs, and passwords. Also known as 'brand spoofing.' An official-looking e-mail is sent to potential victims pretending to be from their ISP, bank, or retail establishment. The e-mail states that due to internal accounting errors or some other pretext, certain information must be updated to continue the service. A link in the message directs the user to a web page that asks for financial information." (TechWeb)

plagiarize. "To steal and pass off the ideas or words of another as one's own; to use another's production without crediting the source; to commit literary theft; to present as new and original an idea or product derived from an existing source." (Merriam-Webster Online Dictionary)

podcasting. "Similar in nature to RSS, which allows users to subscribe to a set of feeds to view syndicated website content. With podcasting, however, you have a set of subscriptions that are checked regularly for updates and instead of reading the feeds on your computer screen, you listen to the new content on your iPod (or like device)." (Webopedia)

RSS (Really Simple Syndication). An XML format for syndicating web content. "A website owner who wants to allow other sites to publish some of his or her site content creates an RSS document and registers the document with an RSS publisher. A user who can read RSS-distributed content can use the content on a different site. Syndicated content includes such data as news feeds, events listings, news stories, headlines, project updates, excerpts from discussion forums, or even corporate information." (Webopedia)

search engine. "Any of a number of giant databases on the Internet that store data on websites and their corresponding URLs. Some popular search engines are Google, Yahoo!, MetaCrawler, AltaVista, and Excite." (4Teachers.org)

spyware. "Any software that covertly gathers user information through the user's Internet connection without his or her knowledge, usually for advertising purposes. Spyware applications are typically bundled as a hidden component of freeware or shareware programs that can be downloaded from the Internet; however, it should be noted that the majority of shareware and freeware applications do not come with spyware. Once installed, the spyware monitors user activity on the Internet and transmits that information in the background to someone else. Spyware can also gather information about e-mail addresses and even passwords and credit card numbers." (Webopedia)

text messaging. "Sending short text messages to a device such as a cellular phone, PDA, or pager. Text messaging is used for messages that are no longer than a few hundred characters. The term is usually applied to messaging that takes place between two or more mobile devices." (Webopedia)

URL (uniform resource locators). "Address of any given site on the Internet." (4Teachers.org)

virtual. "Not real. The term *virtual* is popular among computer scientists and is used in a wide variety of situations. In general, it distinguishes something that is merely conceptual from something that has physical reality. For example, *virtual memory* refers to an imaginary set of locations, or addresses, where data can be stored. It is imaginary in the sense that the memory area is not the same as the real physical memory composed of transistors. The difference is a bit like the difference between an architect's plans for a house and the actual house. A computer scientist might call the plans a *virtual house*. Another analogy is the difference between the brain and the mind. The mind is a *virtual brain*. It exists conceptually, but the actual physical matter is the brain." (Webopedia)

virus. "A program or piece of code that is loaded onto your computer without your knowledge and runs against your wishes. Viruses can also replicate themselves. All computer viruses are manmade. A simple virus that can make a copy of itself over and over again is relatively easy to produce. Even such a simple virus is dangerous because it will quickly use all available memory and bring the system to a halt. An even more dangerous type of virus is one capable of transmitting itself across networks and bypassing security systems." (Webopedia)

web browser. "Computer programs, such as Mozilla Firefox, Apple Safari, Microsoft Internet Explorer, and Mosaic, that help you navigate the web and access text, graphics, hyperlinks, audio, video, and other multimedia. Browsers work by 'translating' or 'interpreting' hypertext markup language (HTML)—the code embedded in web pages that tells them how to look. Browsers read this code and display the web page accordingly." (ClassZone)

wiki. "A collaborative website composed of the perpetual collective work of many authors. Similar to a blog in structure and logic, a wiki allows anyone to edit, delete, or modify content that has been placed on the website using a browser interface, including the work of previous authors. In contrast, a blog, typically authored by an individual, does not allow visitors to change the original posted material, only add comments to the original content. The term *wiki* refers to either the website or the software used to create the site. *Wiki wiki* means 'quick' in Hawaiian." (Webopedia)

wireless. "Telecommunication in which electromagnetic waves (rather than some form of wire) carry the signal over part or all of the communication path." (WhatIs.com)

Sources

4Teachers.org. (2006). *Technology glossary.* Available at www.4teachers.org/techalong/glossary/#a
All definitions from the Tech-along Technology Glossary at 4Teachers.org are © 1995–2006 ALTEC, the University of Kansas. Reprinted with permission.

ClassZone. (No date). Dictionary main page. Available at www.classzone.com

Johnson, D. G., & Nissenbaum, H. (1995). *Computers, ethics & social values.* Upper Saddle River, NJ: Prentice Hall.

Merriam-Webster Online Dictionary. (2008). Dictionary main page. Available at www.merriam-Webster.com
All definitions from Merriam-Webster are © 2007 Merriam-Webster Inc. Reprinted with permission from the Merriam-Webster Online Dictionary (www.merriam-Webster.com).

Occupational and Environmental Health Center. (No date). *Ergonomic technology center.* Available at www.oehc.uchc.edu/ergo.asp

Southern Association of Colleges and Schools. (1996). *Criteria for accreditation.* Decatur, GA: Commission on Colleges.

TechWeb. (1981–2008). Define a term. Available at www.techWeb.com

Webopedia. (2008). Dictionary main page. Available at www.Webopedia.com

WhatIs.com. (2008). Dictionary main page. Available at http://whatis.techtarget.com

Wikipedia. (No date). Encyclopedia main page. Available at www.wikipedia.org

Quick Guide to Popular Technologies

When you're considering buying technology for your children, you'll need to know the advantages and disadvantages associated with that technology. If you are unaware of everything that a technology might or could do, how can you be prepared to help your children? It is not enough to ask, "What does this technology do?" As parents we need to ask, "What can my children do with this technology?" The information presented in this appendix is meant to be a starting place for managing technology in your home. Review the information here and take some time to work with your children so that you can come to a common understanding of what is appropriate and what is not.

MP3 Players

Many MP3 players are now on the market (Clix, iPod, Zune), and most have similar functions—they store information that can be played almost anywhere. Originally they played songs, for the most part, but now they can play videos and audio blogs. To have the best experience with MP3 players, consider the following ideas.

Suggestions

- Identify what the player will be used for—music, movies or videos, books, or podcasts. Will the MP3 player be used mainly for schoolwork or for entertainment?

- Know the type of device that the MP3 will be connected to (most require a connection to some type of computer to collect or transfer files).

- Set some limits on what can be placed on the MP3 player. Discuss your family's values in relation to these materials.

Discussion Points

- How will the media files be gathered? Will they consist of new purchases or be copied from already purchased music? Will the files be downloaded from P2P sites, and, if so, from which sites?

- Talk about copyright issues. If your children place music from CDs on their MP3 players, make sure that the CDs have been purchased, and not shared by others.

- If your children are going to purchase music online, what are the rules and what are the limitations?

- If your children will be using P2P sites, are they aware of the potential dangers? Be sure to discuss adware and spyware, which can infect a computer and collect information to share with others.

Monitor Children's Behavior

- Are your children using the player only when and where MP3 use is appropriate?

- Are they following safety rules and aware of their surroundings when using the player?

- Do they follow basic etiquette when with others and listening to music? (Are they able to hear others? Is the music so loud it's heard outside the earphones?)

- Is the player secured so it won't be stolen? Some MP3 players are expensive and can cost hundreds of dollars, not including the cost of the music or videos on the device.

Gaming Systems

Gaming systems have been around since the 1970s, but today the number of these systems has grown and the quality has increased. Xbox 360, PlayStation (I, II, III), PlayStation Portable (PSP), Nintendo Wii, and Nintendo DS are just a few of the popular examples. Some of these systems are portable, while others are more for home use, but almost all have many options and accessories available. Parents have to be especially careful when looking into these systems.

Suggestions

- If you're thinking about purchasing a gaming system, are you aware of all the associated costs? Games (both purchases and rentals), accessories (additional controllers, special equipment), and subscriptions (online gaming, game rentals) are common add-on expenses.

- Discuss with your children what their expectations are when using these systems. Discover what types of games they want to play, and find out whether they will be playing with friends at home or competing with others online. As they learn more about the system, these expectations may change. You will need to continually talk to your children about how they are using the system.

- Set rules before your children begin using the system. Both you and your children should be comfortable with the rules, and they should be fully understood. Typical rules might include limiting play time, playing with offline real-world friends only, and never chatting with strangers or giving out any personal information (including real name or address).

▪ Educate yourself. Become familiar with game ratings and privacy statements. Review each game before your children play it.

▪ Observe. Check out the games your children play and who they play with. Place the computer or game console in a place where it can be easily monitored.

Discussion Points

▪ Go over the game rating system (E=Everyone, T=Teen, M=Mature) and the nature of games (violence, nudity, fantasy). Discuss whether the values of your family and these games coincide.

▪ Be aware of cyberbullies. Teach your children how to handle bullies in online games.

▪ Choose appropriate names. Have your children use suitable screen or character names (also called gamertags) that follow the rules of the game site. These names should not reveal any personal information or potentially invite harassment.

▪ Teach your kids good online habits. Tell your kids that if they feel uncomfortable with anything that's going on in a game, they should stop playing and tell you about it immediately. You can report the issue if necessary.

▪ Consider the costs associated with purchasing and renting games. How are these going to be paid? By children, by parents, or a mix?

Monitor Children's Behavior

- Monitor game chats and messages. If a player is using inappropriate language, encourage your child to tell you.

- Ensure privacy. Advise your kids when using online gaming chats never to give out any personal information (for example, their name, age, gender, or home address) or pictures of themselves, and never to agree to meet someone in person.

- If the gaming system has the ability to connect to the Internet, it is probably capable of surfing to objectionable sites just like a computer (such as pornography or gambling sites).

Computers

Computers have been in the home for almost 30 years, and the last decade has seen some major changes. With the decrease in cost of laptop computers, children have more access to these convenient devices, as well as greater computing mobility. This is both a good and a bad thing. Kids can write reports on their laptop computers at the library, but they can also do other things—away from adult supervision. Establish ground rules for your children's use of computers. The objective is not only to set boundaries but also to help children understand the reasons why these rules exist so that they can take responsibility for their own actions and develop their own judgment.

Suggestions

- Set limits on when your kids can use the computer and for how long.

- Agree on which types of websites are permissible to visit and which are not.

- Encourage your children to come to you if anything online makes them feel uncomfortable or threatened.

- Make it very clear that they must not give out personal information without your permission, in particular, addresses, phone numbers, school details, passwords, or pictures. Also take care to limit children's access to credit card and bank information.

- Forbid them to meet anyone in person who they encounter online without your consent and without a responsible adult present.

- Restrict their ability to download software, music, or other files without your permission.

- Agree on whether (or not) to allow your kids to spend money online.

- Explain what viruses, spyware, and adware are and what you are doing to prevent them. Ask your kids to come to you if they get an alert while online.

Discussion Points

- Explain that people online are not necessarily who they say they are and that bad people can sometimes appear friendly.

- Discuss how to determine if information found online is accurate and how to spot the difference between fact and opinion.

- Talk about using online resources for homework. It's OK to do research online, but simply cutting and pasting information is plagiarism.

- Explore the nature of Internet piracy—downloading music, television, films, games and other software. Just because sites make files easy to access, it doesn't make it right to take them.

- Discuss how you expect your children to behave toward other people while they are online. Explain that gossiping, bullying, and harassing are unacceptable.

- Talk to your kids about online pornography and direct them to good, age-appropriate sites.

Monitor Children's Behavior

- For younger children, always sit with them while they are online.

- Ask your children to share all their online user names and passwords with you.

- Encourage your children to talk about their Internet experience with you and make it a shared family experience.

- Put computers in an open area in the home rather than in the kids' bedrooms.

- Don't rely on a single technical solution. Supervision and education are also part of good parenting.

Cell Phones

It's becoming more and more common to see kids and cell phones together these days. Parents are finding that by providing cell phones to their kids they are able to keep in better contact with them. In this fast-paced society, being able to contact others with personal communication has become paramount. Unfortunately, cell phones are given to kids with little or no discussion about appropriate and inappropriate use. Take the time to talk with your children about how cell phones should be used.

Suggestions

- Teach your children to excuse themselves when they want to make a call.

- When your kids are anticipating an important call, have them let others know about the call and that they'll need to step away to receive it.

- Cell phones can be a distraction that leads kids to miss out on activities. Talk with your children about how using a cell phone in certain situations can cause them to miss out on family activities.

- Develop cell phone protocol for inside your home. You might want to establish "quiet zones" and "phone-free" areas and times.

- Model appropriate mobile phone use. Children will imitate your actions, just like they do for driving.

Discussion Points

- To begin your discussion, use the following list regarding public places where children should not use their cell phone: libraries, movies, elevators, museums, cemeteries, theaters, dentist or doctor waiting rooms, places of worship, auditoriums, hospital emergency rooms, or public transportation.

- Talk about the type of ringtone they choose. Could it be considered annoying to others?

- Tell your kids not to talk on the cell phone when driving. If it's important, they should find a safe place to pull over and take the call.

- Ask kids to make sure they are at least 10 feet from others when talking on the cell phone.

- Explore when an incoming call should take priority over the situation at hand.

- Talk about what would happen if everyone used their cell phones whenever they wanted. What issues would occur?

- Discuss whether it would be OK to let incoming calls interrupt important family conversations.

Monitor Children's Behavior

- Explain to your children that a cell phone is a tool for safety and parental communication, first and foremost, and not a toy. Allow only those features that children understand how to use appropriately. Additional features can be added later.

- Explain the costs of additional features (such as texting and Internet access). If your children are old enough, have them help pay for these additional features if they want to use them. Keep track of your children's use and go over cell phone bills with them.

- People often leave cell phones and other expensive technologies lying around. Be aware of where your children put their cell phones, and help them to understand that they cannot leave these items unattended (even for a couple of minutes).

- Discuss whether other children will be allowed to use your children's cell phones, and vice versa. Come up with a plan for keeping track of permission.

Family Contract for Digital Citizenship

The following family contract, adapted from SafeKids.com, covers the nine elements of digital citizenship. Divided into a pledge for kids and a pledge for parents, this contract is designed to help individuals understand, discuss, and establish rules for technology use.

Source

SafeKids.com. (No date). *Family contract for online safety.* (Kid's pledge adapted from the brochure *Child safety on the information highway*, by Lawrence J. Magid.) Retrieved August 16, 2008, from http://safekids.com/family-contract-for-online-safety/

Kid's Pledge

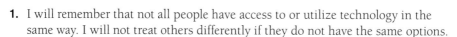

1. I will remember that not all people have access to or utilize technology in the same way. I will not treat others differently if they do not have the same options.

2. I will tell my parents or a responsible adult right away if I come across any information that makes me feel uncomfortable. I understand that to have technology rights I have to be responsible in my actions as well.

3. I will tell my parents if I experience any pain or discomfort when using technology. I will remember that I need to balance technology use with other activities.

4. I will not respond to any messages that are mean or in any way make me feel uncomfortable. It is not my fault if I get a message like that. If I do, I will tell my parents or a responsible adult right away so that they can contact the appropriate groups.

5. I will talk with my parents so that we can set up rules for making purchases online. We will decide if and when online purchases can be made and determine secure sites for me to use.

6. I will treat others the way that I wish to be treated when using technology. I will keep in mind that my technology use affects others.

7. I will check with my parents before downloading or installing software or doing anything that could possibly hurt our computer or jeopardize my family's privacy. I will also keep antivirus, antispyware, and antiadware programs up-to-date to protect our information.

8. I will be a good online citizen and not do anything that hurts other people or is against the law.

9. I will help my parents understand how to have fun and learn things online and teach them things about the Internet, computers, and other technology.

I will help my child follow this agreement, and I will allow reasonable use of digital technology as long as these rules and other family rules are followed.

I agree to the above.

_____
Child's signature

_____
Parent's signature

Parent's Pledge

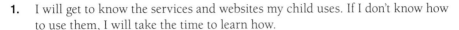

1. I will get to know the services and websites my child uses. If I don't know how to use them, I will take the time to learn how.

2. I will teach my child to understand that other people do not have the same access to technology. I will demonstrate to my child that all technology users should be treated the same.

3. I will work with my child to understand the issues around online purchases. I will show my child which sites are safe and secure for buying goods online. I will also help to explain how to search and find the best deals online.

4. I promise to teach my child when and how to use digital communication methods. I understand that technology may not always be the best way to interact with others.

5. I will help everyone in our family to understand that our technology use affects others. I will help my children to understand they need to act the way they want to be treated.

6. I will try to get to know my child's "online friends" just as I try get to know my child's other friends. I will explain that to have rights online there are certain responsibilities as well.

7. I will teach my child that some material available online is protected and cannot be taken without permission. Children need to understand that this material is owned by others and they have rights to be protected.

8. I will explain to my child that technology needs to be at the proper height for an individual's size to keep from causing physical harm. I will also make sure that my child has limits on the amount of time spent on technology use to avoid addiction to the technology.

9. I will teach my child to protect technology and data by having adequate antivirus, antispyware, and antiadware software. I will also show that having protection is important for all technology.

I agree to the above.

I understand that my parent has agreed to these rules, and I agree to help my parent explore and use technology with me.

_____   _____
Parent's signature   *Child's signature*

National Educational Technology Standards for Students (NETS·S)

The National Educational Technology Standards for Students are divided into six broad categories. Standards within each category are to be introduced, reinforced, and mastered by students. Educators can use these standards as guidelines for planning technology-based activities in which students achieve success in learning, communication, and life skills. For more information on the NETS Project, visit www.iste.org/nets.

1. **Creativity and Innovation**

    Students demonstrate creative thinking, construct knowledge, and develop innovative products and processes using technology. Students:

    a. apply existing knowledge to generate new ideas, products, or processes

    b. create original works as a means of personal or group expression

    c. use models and simulations to explore complex systems and issues

    d. identify trends and forecast possibilities

2. Communication and Collaboration

Students use digital media and environments to communicate and work collaboratively, including at a distance, to support individual learning and contribute to the learning of others. Students:

a. interact, collaborate, and publish with peers, experts, or others employing a variety of digital environments and media

b. communicate information and ideas effectively to multiple audiences using a variety of media and formats

c. develop cultural understanding and global awareness by engaging with learners of other cultures

d. contribute to project teams to produce original works or solve problems

3. Research and Information Fluency

Students apply digital tools to gather, evaluate, and use information. Students:

a. plan strategies to guide inquiry

b. locate, organize, analyze, evaluate, synthesize, and ethically use information from a variety of sources and media

c. evaluate and select information sources and digital tools based on the appropriateness to specific tasks

d. process data and report results

4. Critical Thinking, Problem Solving, and Decision Making

Students use critical-thinking skills to plan and conduct research, manage projects, solve problems, and make informed decisions using appropriate digital tools and resources. Students:

a. identify and define authentic problems and significant questions for investigation

b. plan and manage activities to develop a solution or complete a project

c. collect and analyze data to identify solutions and make informed decisions

d. use multiple processes and diverse perspectives to explore alternative solutions

5. **Digital Citizenship**

Students understand human, cultural, and societal issues related to technology and practice legal and ethical behavior. Students:

  a. advocate and practice the safe, legal, and responsible use of information and technology

  b. exhibit a positive attitude toward using technology that supports collaboration, learning, and productivity

  c. demonstrate personal responsibility for lifelong learning

  d. exhibit leadership for digital citizenship

6. **Technology Operations and Concepts**

Students demonstrate a sound understanding of technology concepts, systems, and operations. Students:

  a. understand and use technology systems

  b. select and use applications effectively and productively

  c. troubleshoot systems and applications

  d. transfer current knowledge to the learning of new technologies